a generation
CHOSEN

Ben Courson

But you are a chosen generation, a royal priesthood, a holy nation, His own special people, that you may proclaim the praises of Him who called you out of darkness into His marvelous light.

– 1 Peter 2:9

Table of Contents

Introduction 7

Jesus is My Homeboy? 11

From the T-shirt to the Bible 13

The Body of Christ Can't Do the Splits 15

If You Walk Into a Garage, Does That Make You a Car? 20

Satan's Deadliest Weapon: NyQuil 24

The Great Delete Button 29

His Body for Our Bodies 35

Lust is a Pop Quiz, Not Just an SAT 41

Cassandra and Jamal 46

A Dungeon of Dreamers 53

If Not Now, When? 56

God's Promises are Not for Window Shoppers 61

You May Have Sunk . . . But At Least You Walked On Water 66

Superheroes 73

David and the Grasshopper 79

Whom the Lord Loveth He Kicketh 88

Know God, No Fear. No God, Know Fear. 94

Empty Superstars 102

The Answer to Every Problem 106

Introduction

I love it when you're at a concert and the lead singer tells everyone to take out their cell phones and hold them up. Hundreds and hundreds of glowing screens fill the room. You look out at the crowd and it's as if each person has a star in their hand, contributing to the glittering galaxy that was created through the simple word that was spoken by the singer.

The Lord, just like the lead singer, created the universe's shining galaxies simply by *speaking* them into existence. But not only that, He has made *you and me* like the stars above the moment we became Christians. Now He literally calls us the "light of the world." And in Matthew 5:16, Jesus invited us to bust out our cell phones and start glowing for Him when He said, "Let your light so shine before men that they may see your good works and glorify your Father in Heaven."

I so badly want this generation to glow like that beautiful galaxy of cell phones. I so badly want us to get our light out of our pocket and start holding it up for everyone to see. And I want the world to be *attracted* to Jesus when they see us shine. And that is why I wrote this book . . .

The funny thing is, the title *A Generation Chosen* doesn't seem like a very personal title. It sounds like this would be a book written to a collective group of people rather than to the individual. But the truth is, I wrote this book for the individual. The truths on these pages are deeply personal, and I want them to reach *your* heart. In order to see our *generation* glowing brightly for Jesus, *each individual* must play their part.

Think about it. If I'm standing next to you at the concert, and the lead singer tells me to take out my cell phone and hold it up, if I didn't charge my phone before I got there, then I'm not going to have any light to add to the beauty of the room. Just because *you* charged your phone doesn't mean *my* phone will glow. I must individually charge it up, and you must individually charge yours up, so we can glow *together*. So too, your parents and friends may shine for the Lord. But you can't depend on their glow. *You've* got to get charged up in God's presence individually if you want to add light and beauty to this chosen generation.

My hope is that this book will be a power socket you can plug into to get your light charged up. So because each generation speaks a different language than the previous one, I wrote this book as if I were just talking to a friend. This is written specifically for my peers, for other young people. Because I figure I'm not going to be young for very long, I wanted to take advantage of this opportunity to speak to the youth while I'm still one of them. But even though this book is written with that purpose in mind, if you are not in the category of "youth" any longer, I would be honored for you to read this book anyways. Firstly to catch a glimpse of what the Lord is up to in the lives of the young people that you're linked to (your kids or nephews or students). But secondly because the truths I discuss are from Scripture. And Scripture is timeless. And its truths relate to us regardless of our age.

One more thing I want to add in this introduction. This book is set up like a roller coaster ride. Some chapters are intended to lift us high up into hope. Others are meant to bring us low in humility and repentance. My goal is that we would be ridiculously convicted at the beginning and absurdly happy by the end of this ride. So I've got to warn you. The first five chapters in particular are very challenging ones, which are meant to instill the fear of God in us. But by chapter 6, the high hope starts kicking in. Strewn through the pages are some of my most personal stories and some of the ones I think are the funniest to help us grasp the exciting truths we will be discussing.

I want to thank you for joining me on this ride. Now let's buckle up and see where this roller coaster will take us!

Chapter 1

Jesus is My Homeboy?

A few years ago, when I was in high school, I remember walking into a store with my mom and sister and seeing for the first time a t-shirt which said, "Jesus is my Homeboy." I wasn't a big fan of shopping or looking at clothes then, but this shirt grabbed hold of my attention and wouldn't let go. Why was this article of clothing so fascinating to me?

Several years went by and "Jesus is my Homeboy" clothes got really popular for a while. I haven't seen any more of those shirts or hats for some time, but the phrase has stuck with me.

Jesus is my homeboy.

Hmm. I think the reason this has been swirling around in my head is because it's really a perfect description of who our generation thinks Jesus is. A hippie with long hair who holds up a peace sign and offers His love to anyone who says a magic sinner's prayer. "Jesus is my friend, man!" says the guy who walks out of the party slightly drunk. "Accepted Him into my heart years ago. He's my Lord and Savior!"

Really?

Is that what it means to be a Christian? It doesn't really matter how you live, as long as you "accept Him into your heart" and claim Him as your Savior? Tragically, this is what so many young people believe. And my heart breaks when I think about just how many of them say "Jesus is my friend" only to one day hear *Him* say, "Depart from Me, I never knew you."

So I decided to write this book. A message is burning in my bones, and I've got to let it out. Our generation must dig through the ruins of contemporary thinking and unearth the Jesus of the Bible. And when we as youth discover Jesus for ourselves, our lives will never be the same.

The thing is, since I'm writing this as a twenty-two year old, I'm just one youth calling out to you, another youth, to rediscover God and make our lives count. In order to do that, we've got to think for ourselves and dig up the ancient truths in fresh ways. So I can't stroke my long white beard, peer through small spectacles, and utter wise sayings that will change your life. I obviously don't have that ability. I just want to invite you to join with me on an adventure to discover what Jesus wants to be for the youth of the twenty-first century. Every generation the Holy Ghost moves in a new way, so please don't just settle for your parents' faith. Don't simply believe what they believe. Own Jesus for yourself. We are a new generation. A chosen generation. But we're not going to be young forever. So this is our chance to rise to our fate. This is our chance to rebel against the status quo and forever change our world.

Chapter 2

From the T-shirt to the Bible

I love how Jesus never waters anything down.

On one page He will say something wildly challenging, and then on the next page He will say something absurdly hopeful. One minute He says if your hand is causing you to sin, chop it off. The next minute He says you can pray for anything, and if you believe you'll receive it, you will have it.

Jesus is the ultimate Revolutionary. Nothing He said was ordinary. He was so drastic in everything He said and did that sometimes just reading His words make us nervous.

Don't you just love that about Him?

A lot of times, though, we understandably feel the need to explain Jesus away. We've got to give Him some moderation! Sometimes He's a little extreme for our taste. I mean, let's face it, it's easier to let Jesus be the safe hippie on the t-shirt, because that Jesus is much safer than the Biblical Jesus. But in a generation racked by moral depravity, we could really use His fierce challenges right about now. And in a day when depression runs rampant and unchecked, we could really use some of His "idealistic" hope too. The Jesus of the Bible offers them both. He doesn't offer a life of ease, but of adventure. Of risk. Of destiny.

It's time for the youth to return to child-like faith and take His wildly hopeful promises at face value. It's also time for us to embrace the challenge of rediscovering the lost concept of fearing the Lord. And I'm convinced, if we embrace both extremities, the hope *and* the challenge, they will naturally balance themselves out.

Ralph Waldo Emerson once said, "Always do what you are afraid to do." To be honest, it's scary to hope. We're all afraid of disillusionment and getting our hopes up. And it's also scary to be challenged. It's frightening when God holds up the mirror, shows us our flaws, and summons us to greatness.

So because it's scary to hope, and because it's scary to embrace the challenge, I suggest we do them both.

Chapter 3

The Body of Christ Can't Do the Splits

Could you imagine what our generation would look like if we took Jesus' words at face value? If we really believed what He said was absolute truth? For example, when Jesus said, "You cannot serve two masters," could you fathom how much different the Church would be if we took this to heart? Yet so many young people don't believe this. They believe they *can* serve two masters. Some days they're serving worldly pleasure, other days they're serving the Lord. On Sunday morning they use their lips to praise Jesus, but then on Friday night they press those same lips to the beer can as they kiss the Enemy. On Wednesday night they'll study the Bible in youth group, but then the next day at school they gossip, cuss, and show partiality to the popular kids.

This is one of the most tragic things taking place in the youth today. A lot of people assume they can serve the Enemy *and* Jesus. But it's impossible. Can a person serve two opposite masters who give contradicting commands? Yet still people try to play on Satan's team one day and God's the next. But they fail to realize that in trying to win it all, they're losing their soul.

It's absurd to attempt to play for two teams simultaneously. Trust me, I know this well. When I was in eighth grade, I played for the South Medford Generals AAU basketball team. I'll never forget the first game of the season. I couldn't have been more nervous as the game was about to begin. The ref tossed the ball in the air to commence a new season, and it was tipped right to me. First play of the game, and the ball was in my hands. I dribbled furiously to the basket, but as I did so I noticed the defenders weren't guarding me. They were just staring at me. I couldn't figure out why they'd let me shoot uncontested, but I went up for the lay-up anyways. I laid the ball off the glass, and it fell through the net. *Yes! First five seconds of the season, and I already have two points!* I felt like the man.

But the stands were eerily quiet. No one was cheering. I looked over at my coaches, and their faces showed dismay. I didn't even get a "Good job, Benny!" from my mom. Then I knew something was wrong. Very wrong. I looked up at the scoreboard, and we were down by two. First play of the *season,* and I scored for the wrong team!

Now, what if I went up to my coach and, rather than apologizing for my ridiculous blunder, I said, "You know, Coach, I kinda like playing for both teams. So how about this, sometimes I'll shoot on our hoop and sometimes I'll shoot on theirs." Do you think he'd keep me in the game a second longer? Of course not! He'd sideline me because I'd be doing my team more harm than good.

So too, Jesus said, "Anyone who isn't helping Me opposes Me, and anyone who isn't working with Me is actually working against Me." Either you're on Jesus' team or you're not. If you try to play for both teams simultaneously, you will do Him more harm than good. That's why, honestly, it's better to say you're not a Christian than live for God sometimes and for sin at other times. Christians who live double lives just drag Jesus' name through the mud. It breaks my heart, but I constantly hear the main reason young people don't want to walk with the Lord is because they think Christians are hypocrites. They think Christians are fake, acting one way at church but a completely different way the moment they walk out the sanctuary doors. Sadly, most of the time they're right.

It's time to turn this thing around. As a new generation of Christians, let's represent the name of Christ well. There's a reason we're called the Body of Christ. We're to be a mirror reflection of how Jesus lived when He was in His earthly body. When Jesus' literal body was ascending up to Heaven, it's as if He looked down at His followers and said, "I'm leaving the earth now. It's your turn to be My body." Until He returns, we are now the physical, tangible representation of Christ to the world. Are we mirroring Him accurately? Or have we cast a distorted reflection of who He really is?

Let me tell you this, we're *never* going to reflect Jesus accurately if we're trying to do the splits. Let me explain. I'm the least flexible person in the world. As a high schooler, when I was tested for sit-and-reach, I got a negative twelve. A *negative* twelve. That means I was twelve centimeters away from even reaching the starting point! So if you tried to make me do the splits, I would break. The Body of Christ is like that. We can't do the spiritual splits. If we're trying to put one foot in the world and one foot in Christianity, both feet will be pulled so hard in opposite directions that we'll literally break.

James said it well when he declared, "You adulterers! Don't you realize that friendship with the world makes you an enemy of God? I say it again, that if your aim is to enjoy the world, you can't be a friend of God." Whose friend are you? Does your life show that you're a friend of God? Or have you befriended the worldly pleasures and sins that have so grossly infiltrated our generation?

Several months ago I was in a youth service where the worship leader sang, "I am a friend of God." I thought the song was passionate and beautiful. And it's an inspiring anthem to sing. But when we really stop to think about what it means to be a friend of the Lord, we'll find it's very different than the "Jesus is my Homeboy" slogan. Jesus told His disciples this: "You are My friends if you obey Me." He didn't say, "You're My friend if your t-shirt says so," or

"You're My friend if you invite Me into your heart." Jesus never said that. He told His disciples their friendship must be proved by their obedience.

It makes a lot of sense why He'd say that. Think of it this way. Imagine I came up to you, put my arm around your shoulder, and told you you're my best friend in the whole world. But what if right after I said that, I punched you in the face, elbowed you in the stomach, kicked you in the shins, then walked away? Would you believe what I said? Obviously you'd say, "You're crazy Ben! You might say I'm your friend, but the way you treat me proves the opposite." It's one thing to claim you and Jesus are friends, but the real question is do you treat Him as one?

Because when you really stop to think about it, our sin is the very thing that literally beat up Jesus and put Him on the cross. He wasn't crucified because He was an insubordinate revolutionary who threatened the Roman Empire. No. The Bible says He willingly laid down His life in order to pay for *our* sins. That means every time I dishonor my parents *I* am the one holding the javelin, piercing His side. Every time I gossip, *I'm* the one forcing the crown of thorns on His head. Every time I lose my temper, *my* fist is the one striking Jesus' face. So how could I call Him "friend" if I don't even care when I do the very things that murdered Him?

Honestly, it means nothing to say you and Jesus are friends. I can claim that me and President Obama are really close. But that doesn't mean we are. I could tell you he's my friend all I want, but if I went up to him, gave him a friendly slug on the arm and said, "Long time no see Barack! How's it going, old buddy old pal? How's the kids?" He'd lean over to his wife and whisper, "Do I even know this guy?" I might say the president is *my* friend, but that doesn't mean I'm *his* friend. Anyone can say, "Jesus is my friend!" But what really counts is whether or not Jesus would agree with you.

"But I *know* the Lord is my friend," many say, "I know it because I believe in Him!" But even the demons believe in God. Does that mean *they* are saved? The Apostle James said if you believe in God but can't prove it by your works, your faith is dead. He didn't say your faith is weak. Or needs improvement. He said it's dead.

Having faith without good deeds is like driving home from school and seeing a homeless man on the side of the road. You can see he's hungry and cold, and you know you should do something for him. So you call out to him from your car, "God bless you brother! Stay warm and be filled!" But that's all you do. You don't feed him or give him a jacket, so you let him starve and freeze to death. Your religious and "kind" words mean nothing. In the same way, it isn't enough just to say, "God, I believe in You!" You've got to back it up. We can say Christian things and profess Jesus with our words, but if our actions can't prove our claims, our relationship with God is as dead as our faith.

Chapter 4

If You Walk Into a Garage, Does That Make You a Car?

So how would you live your life if you knew you were being recorded 24/7 by a hidden video camera; filming you while you were at school . . . at home with your family . . . all by yourself? Would you talk differently? Treat your little brother differently? Use your computer differently? The reality is, there *is* a camera, a heavenly one, that records every moment of your life. The Bible says everything is naked and exposed before the eyes of the God to whom we must explain all that we have done. His eyes work like video cameras, recording everything. Although we can't remember 99% of our sins, God remembers all of them. He may be the "Ancient of Days," but He doesn't get Alzheimer's. And one day He will reach into His flawless memory bank and pull out the tape which tells your life story. He will pop it into the heavenly TV, press play, and you will have to give an account for your actions.

Are you prepared to meet your God?

If you died today, are you really ready to stand before the Judge of both the living and the dead? On that day you won't be able to point your finger at your husband and say, "Well he did worse things than me!" You won't be able to look at the crowd and declare, "But Lord, everyone was doing it!" You can't bring anyone else into it. It's just going to be you and God. He won't ask you to explain the actions of others: you'll only be called upon to answer for one person - yourself.

And your account will be a *personal* account. That means you can't bring your mom and dad with you. Their faith won't save you. Just because they may follow the Lord, teach you the Bible, and drive you to church doesn't mean you have a faith of your own. You can't have a personal, saving faith in Jesus through your parents. "But Ben," you say, "I don't just have Christian parents, my group of friends are all Christians too!" You may hang around believers all the time, but can *their* relationship with Jesus make *you* right with God? You may even go to church every week, but as Billy Sunday would say, "Going to church doesn't make you a Christian any more than going to a garage makes you an automobile." I never walk into a garage and think, "I must be a car." Yet many people walk into a church building, sit in the sanctuary, and think that means they're Christians. The only way you'll be saved is if you own your relationship with God. You can't rely on the faith of your mom, a friend, or your pastor. So let me ask you a really tough question: is the Lord so real to you that even if everyone in the world stopped believing and somehow "proved" that God doesn't exist, you would still believe?

Tragically, Jesus taught that many are going to knock on the door of Heaven and say, "Lord, Lord, didn't we prophesy in Your name? Didn't we use Your name to drive out demons and perform many miracles? Won't You let us in?" But He will tell them, "I never knew you. Away from Me, you evildoers!" You can approach the door of Heaven and pound as hard as you want until your "Jesus is my Homeboy" hat falls off, but that won't open the gates of Heaven for you. You can tell the Lord you were a "good" person, spout off a bunch of religious words, and explain to Him that your parents faithfully took you to church. You can remind Jesus you listed Him as one of your heroes on your MySpace page. But that won't save you. Only if your faith is really yours, demonstrating itself through good deeds, will you hear Jesus say, "Well done, good and faithful servant! Come, enter into the joy of the Lord."

Are you positive He will say that to you? Or have the temptations of the world been sucking you away from your commitment to Him? Do whatever it takes . . . *whatever* it takes, to make sure you belong to Him. Work hard to *prove* that you really are among those whom God has chosen. Jesus would even go so far as to say, "If your hand or foot causes you to sin, cut it off and throw it away. It is better to enter Heaven crippled or lame than to be thrown into the unquenchable fire with both of your hands and feet." I agree with Him!

What if the doctor told you that you had a disease in your hand, and if you didn't amputate your arm, the disease would spread throughout your body and kill you? Would you say, "Don't worry, Doc! You're making way too big a deal out of this small disease. There's no way I'm getting rid of my arm!" How foolish that would be! It definitely isn't easy to amputate your arm, but it's a lot better to live with one arm than die with two. Nor is it easy to get rid of sin . . . sometimes it's so painful it feels like you're cutting off a limb! But sin is a fatal disease, and if you don't chop it off now, it will spread. "Well I'll only go one step further with my girlfriend," you say, "then I'll stop." Famous last words. You think you can get away with giving in to just a little more sin. You think you can escape unscathed. But you never can.

Repent while you still have the chance.

"Hold on Ben," you say, "you're being a little extreme. Slow down. I agree that sin is a disease of sorts, but don't be so intense! All things done in moderation." Let me ask you a question. Should evil *ever* be done in moderation? If you saw someone put two little drops of poison into the very healthy bowl of Lucky Charms I was about to have for breakfast, wouldn't you be extreme in warning me? Wouldn't you make me dump out the *whole* bowl? If I said, "Relax. Let me at least eat some of my cereal in peace. I'm sure I can eat around the poison. Besides, it's only a couple drops." You would grab the bowl and chuck it against the wall before I could take a single bite. Just a little poison is lethal. So too, just a little bit of sin may seem harmless, but it's deadly. Dump it *all* out. "Except you repent," Jesus said, "you shall all perish."

But the Devil's greatest trick is to make us believe that we can put off getting rid of our sin. "You're young. There's no hurry!" he whispers into your ear. "Don't worry, you'll do the right thing after you have a little fun and get a taste of the world." The Father of Lies indeed! The Devil knows if he can get us to procrastinate, then victory is his.

One of the main reasons I got a 2.0 GPA in my core classes my sophomore year was because I procrastinated. I wanted to have fun first and do homework later. But how right was Martin Luther when he said, "How soon 'not now' becomes 'never'." So too, you may think you will get around to cutting off your sin. But there's no time for delay. The Bible says life is like a morning fog; it appears for a moment but evaporates suddenly and unexpectedly. You have no idea what day will be your last. I've seen the reality of this truth first hand. When I was eight years old, my own sister, who loved Jesus with all of her heart, went home to be with the Lord. She was eager and ready to meet her Savior. She was sixteen.

You may be young . . . but you are not invincible. Are you prepared to die? If you met Jesus face to face right now, would He call you His friend, or would He tell you He doesn't know you? With every breath you breathe you're one step closer to meeting your Maker. Your time is running out.

Chapter 5

Satan's Deadliest Weapon: NyQuil

It scares me. When I think of the great and challenging truths of the Bible, I get frightened. But I'm not so sure that's a bad thing. Maybe when the Bible says we're supposed to fear God it actually means we're supposed to fear God. I think a healthy fear of the Lord is precisely what our generation needs right now.

Jesus relayed a very terrifying message to the Church of Laodicea in Revelation 3 because they had lost their fear of God. They'd become lukewarm. Uncaring. Sleepy in their faith. So Jesus told them that if they didn't repent He would spit them out of His mouth. He didn't say He would rebuke them. Or give them a time-out. He said He'd vomit them out. Could there be a scarier fate than that?

Living a half-hearted Christian life is nothing but a lose-lose. It's really pretty pointless if you think about it. When a person is halfway committed to Jesus, not only are they jeopardizing eternity, but they're going to be miserable in life too. The saying is true - they have too much of the Lord in them to enjoy the world, and too much of the world in them to enjoy the Lord. They don't even have that much fun sinning because the "Christian" in them feels guilty. And they don't like going to church because the worldly part of them would rather go out and party.

But you know what is one of the most tragic things about these luke-warm people? They don't even realize that lukewarm Christianity is actually the most dangerous religion of all. They're sleep walking off of a cliff. Jesus told the Laodicean Church that they were wretched, miserable, blind and naked . . . but they didn't even know it. They thought they were safe. They had no clue the Lord was about to spit them out. They were the most comfortable people in the world! But little did they know, Jesus was disgusted by the taste of their lifestyles.

I think this is why I'm not a big fan of coffee. I remember when I was a kid, I walked into my bedroom one morning and saw a white mug. I thought it was a glass of water so I picked it up and took a sip. "Ugh!" I thought. "What is this stuff?" I looked into the cup and saw it was lukewarm coffee that had been left in my room by accident. To this day I don't drink coffee because it only reminds me of that gross room temperature taste.

Jesus hates the taste of room temperature Christians. He doesn't want a mixture of hot and cold: people who are on fire for Him one moment but have a cold heart toward Him the next. Part of the reason He finds lukewarm living sickening is because halfway committed disciples tear down the Kingdom of God more than build it up. See, when we are hot for the Lord, the world will love the taste of Jesus they get every time they're around us (like hot coffee on a cold morning), and they'll want more! Even if we're cold toward the Lord and denounce His name, at least people won't get a wrong taste of Jesus, because no one can drink solid ice! But when we're lukewarm, we portray Jesus wrongly and people will hate the taste of Christianity.

Lukewarm believers make more people want to stay away from Christ than come to Him. They give Christianity a bad name because of their mask-juggling act. They have a tendency to be eight different people in one day. They talk a certain way at church but change their vocabulary the moment they walk into the gym. They discuss the Bible with Christian friends but then tell terrible jokes around unbelievers. They have all these different faces they put on: the tough face around their athlete friends, the church face around Christians, the "cool" face around the partiers. But in time they get exhausted trying to juggle all their masks. It gets really tricky for them when they're hanging out with two unbelievers, and then two church friends walk up and join the conversation. They panic and think, "Oh no! Which face am I supposed to wear now? Am I supposed to be the Christian or the sinner?" They know deep down they can't maintain their multiple identities forever.

If we want to win our generation for Christ, then we've got to relinquish the masks. We are to have one face. A Christian face. Everywhere we go, our countenance should be glowing and attracting people to the Lord. Kind of like Moses. The Bible says that when this great man of God spent forty days in the Lord's presence, his face literally started glowing. Like a light bulb. And when the children of Israel saw him, they wanted to follow him and do whatever he told them to do. When we let our face shine brightly, people will see our godliness and *want* to follow us as we follow Christ.

Growing up, my parents taught us kids to shine bright for Jesus 24/7. Christianity doesn't have an "on" and "off" switch. We're to always be "on" fire for Him. So whenever we asked for permission to hang out in an atmosphere where unbelievers were, I love what my Dad said. He told us we could . . . on one condition - if we were thermostats and not thermometers. It's one of the best pieces of advice I've ever heard. A thermostat sets the temperature of a room. It changes the atmosphere because it sets the standard. A thermometer, on the other hand, rises and drops depending on the atmosphere you put it in. Jesus was able to hang out with sinners because He was a thermostat. *He* was the One who set the standard, therefore He didn't change when He was around sinners . . . He was the One who changed *them!* When you're a thermostat, you'll be just as sold out for Jesus on Friday night, when you're in a worldly atmosphere, as you are when you're at church Sunday morning. A thermometer Christian, though, will have a high degree of passion for the Lord only when they're hanging out with believers, but their passion drops drastically when you put them in a worldly setting. They're hot for God when they're around on-fire believers, room temperature around lukewarm Christians, and cold toward God when they're hanging out with frozen-hearted unbelievers. Their degree of holiness is determined by their surroundings.

Do you change the spiritual temperature of any room you walk into, or are you changed by the existing spiritual temperature of the room? Are you hot for God one moment but then show Him the cold shoulder the next? Don't say it's just your personality to change around people. Don't say you're naturally a follower. Be a different kind of follower. A follower of Jesus. You don't have to be a room temperature, thermometer Christian any longer. Don't keep "sort of" walking with Him. There's no room for sleepy Christianity in the Kingdom of God.

So here is a wake up call for the soul. The alarm clock is going off. Don't press snooze. The Bible says Satan is on the prowl looking for victims he can devour. If we don't wake up and go on the watch right now, we'll be done for.

There was one youth who found this out the hard way. His name was Eutychus. There he was, sitting on the windowsill as Paul the Apostle preached late into the night. The low-ceilinged room was lit by many flickering candles, and the cozy atmosphere combined with the body heat of the people made Eutychus sleepy. In the middle of Paul's message, around midnight, he couldn't keep his heavy eyelids open any longer. He nodded off and fell into a deep sleep.

As the z's floated above his head, he fell out the window and plummeted three stories to his death.

Like Eutychus, young people are falling left and right. They're plummeting to their deaths. And the most dangerous weapon the Enemy is using to destroy our generation is not drugs, drinking parties, or pornography. The deadliest weapon Satan's using is spiritual Nyquil. If he can get us to become sleepy in our faith, we'll end up as defenseless prey in his jaws. If he can lull us to a drowsy, safe, half-hearted Christianity, he'll push us out the window.

Our surroundings are cozy and comfortable, just like Eutychus'. We have Xbox, Facebook, and movie theatres. Cars, Doritos, and flat-screen TV's. We live better than kings used to live, but our comfortable surroundings are making us fall asleep to the things of God. The night is getting late, and as the spiritual darkness grows, so does our sleepiness. And little do we know, we're right where the Devil wants us to be. This is a matter of life or death. We've got to wake up.

But maybe you're reading this and you've already plummeted to your death. You've fallen away from God. You say, "It's too late for me. I've been the lukewarm person who's been half-hearted in my faith, and now I'm dead spiritually." I have good news for you: it's not over yet. Eutychus' story didn't end that night. After he fell and died, Paul rushed out to see him, embraced his dead body . . . and the boy came back to life!

It's time for a resurrection. No matter how sleepy or dead your Christianity has become, if you'll come into Jesus' embrace, you too will come back to life. This isn't the end for you. Heed the call. There is still hope.

Chapter 6

The Great Delete Button

"Wow," you say, "I hope there's hope because I feel pretty convicted after what I've read." Good. I feel the same way. Every time I consider the Bible's severe challenges in conjunction with my failure to meet them, my conscience gets stricken. It drives me crazy whenever I think back over all my stupidity. That's why I wish so badly life gave me delete buttons . . .

You know when you're typing and your eyes are focused on something other than your computer, so you finally look up at your screen but discover all the words you typed were misspelled because your fingers were just a little off home row? That happens to me sometimes, and it's pretty frustrating. But the cool thing about computers is, unlike typewriters, whenever you mess up you can just press the delete button and your spelling errors are gone forever.

I wish I could do that in life. I wish I had a Great Delete Button that could somehow magically erase all my mistakes. "Ah man, I shouldn't have said that!" *Delete.* "Ugh . . . why did I treat him so badly?" *Delete.* "I knew I shouldn't have given in to that temptation!" *Delete.* How cool would that be?

Too bad life doesn't do that. Our errors are permanent and they stick out like a sore thumb. There's nothing we can do to take them back. If only we could just start life all over again! So many times I've wished I could take the knowledge I have now, go back in time, become a kid again and correct all my mistakes. But I can't.

And that leaves me hopeless.

All the ridiculous things I've done and idle words I've spoken have been caught on tape by the "Heavenly Camera." That means I'm toast. You're toast too.

So what in the world are we supposed to do?

This is where the best news the world has ever known comes in. Jesus' blood is the Great Delete Button we've all been longing for. It can *literally* erase our mistakes from God's flawless memory bank. All the bad scenes of my life story that have been filmed by His eyes can finally be edited out!

"How do you know that?" you ask. "Are you just making that up?" No. Listen to what the Lord promised His people once the New Covenant was in play: "I will never again remember their sins and lawless deeds." Isn't it mind-boggling that God has the power not only to forgive, but also *forget* our sins? Because of the Blood of the New Covenant, I *can* become a kid again and go back to correct all my mistakes . . . Jesus told me I can actually be *born again.*

What beautiful news! It's no wonder Paul the Apostle declared to the Church at Corinth, "When I first came to you I didn't use lofty words and brilliant ideas to tell you God's message. For I decided to concentrate only on Jesus Christ and His death on the cross." Paul was a brilliant scholar. A genius really. But out of all the mind-blowing, eloquent messages he could have given, he chose to focus on the simplicity of Jesus' cross.

"But I already know the message of the cross," you say. I too have known this message since I was a little kid. But more than ever I realize this: I need the cross just as much today as I did the first day I came to Christ. In fact, the older I get the more I feel like I need it! But whenever I push the cross to the back of my mind, whenever I think its message is for baby Christians, my guilt will start to paralyze me again. After I mess up I begin to feel the severe reality of Isaiah's words when he said, "There is a problem - your sins have cut you off from God."

A problem indeed! But when I revisit the cross, I remember that that problem has been solved. Once and for all.

On the tree, the Son stretched out one arm to grab the Father's hand, and the other arm to grab my hand, and like a butterfly curl He pulled the weight of the world and brought me and God together. Now nothing, nothing in all the world, can separate me from Him.

"Wait a minute," you say. "What about the last few chapters I read? Does this absurdly hopeful reality that Jesus' blood can delete my mistakes nullify the fierce Biblical challenges we've been discussing?" Of course not! The hope and the challenge still coexist. In fact, they *must* coexist. The psalmist understood how the hopeful reality of forgiveness and the challenge of godliness can work together. He declared, "LORD, if you kept a record of our sins, who O Lord, could ever survive? But You offer forgiveness, that we might learn to fear You." He didn't say, "You offer forgiveness, that we might learn to sin more." No. He said the Lord forgives *so that we might learn to fear Him.* A lot of young people know God offers forgiveness, they just leave out the "fearing Him" part.

I recently read this quote by Emo Philips that sums up the mindset of so much of the youth today: "When I was a kid I used to pray every night for a new bicycle. Then I realized that the Lord doesn't work that way so I stole one and asked Him to forgive me." I think we've all been there before. Asking God to pardon us *before* we commit the crime. But some people live their whole lives this way. They abuse grace, using it as nothing more than an excuse to keep on sinning. But the Bible knows nothing of this kind of forgiveness.

Imagine your parents go away for the weekend. They leave the keys in your hand and tell you the house is yours while they're gone. "There's only one rule," they say, "don't have anyone over while we're gone." You smile and nod your head in agreement, but the moment they walk out the door you snatch your cell phone out of your pocket and begin calling everyone you know. You invite them to the huge party you'll be throwing in a few hours. So that night a hundred people come over. You're just living it up while there's drinking, drugs, and dirty dancing going on. Your parents come home a few days later and find out what you've done. You know you're busted. You'll probably be grounded for life. But you're shocked when they say, with tears in their eyes, "We forgive you."

In that moment you will do one of two things. You'll either be amazed at the love of your parents, and heart-broken over what you've done. You'll never want to do it again. Or you'll act like your sorry, but inwardly you're thinking, "Sweet! I can't believe they just forgave me . . . I never realized how gracious they are. I gotta find out when they're leaving again so I can throw another party!"

Sadly, this is how a lot of people treat the grace of God. "Sweet! Jesus forgives me . . . I guess that means I can keep on living it up!" It's true the Lord is more gracious than we could ever fathom. He is quick to forgive, and He *wants* to delete our sins. But He's God. And He will not be mocked. You can't toy with Him and get away with it.

King David knew how forgiveness is to be received. With a broken heart. After he had an affair with Bathsheba and murdered her husband to cover up his sin, he prayed, "The sacrifice You want is a broken spirit. A broken and repentant heart, O God, You will not despise." After we sin, the Lord is not desiring outward repentance that looks pious. He's looking for a heart that is sincerely remorseful. A heart that won't abuse His grace.

You offer forgiveness, that we might learn to fear You.

Did you know the Bible says, "The fear of the LORD is to hate evil"? That is one of its definitions. Fearing God means you abhor sin so much you get a baby barf every time you think about it. Can we really say we *hate* sin? Or are we entertained by wicked shows? Do we laugh at the perverse jokes?

How can we judge others for not "accepting" God's grace and forgiveness if we're abusing it ourselves? It's no wonder Christian hypocrisy drives unbelievers nuts. We claim forgiveness, but we don't fear the Lord. We preach about Jesus, but we have "Sympatico El Diablo" written all over us . . .

I'll never forget it. It was one of the most embarrassing messages I'd ever given. We had just started a service on Saturday night with loud worship, and I was *so* excited about it. For one of the first services I had this new shirt I really wanted to wear. It had Spanish words on it with really cool font, but I hadn't taken the time to interpret what the words meant. So that night I taught the Bible wearing this shirt all the while. A week later, a friend told me in passing that my shirt said "Sympatico El Diablo." In English that means Sympathy for the Devil. One of the first Saturday night services ever and I'm preaching with a "Sympathy for the Devil" shirt on!

We do that sometimes in life. When we preach to people, rather than covering our hearts with the breastplate of righteousness, we put on the Sympatico El Diablo shirt. People are reading us. They're reading our life story to see if it lines up with the message we're sharing. And they won't listen to our message of forgiveness if we're not fearing God ourselves.

It's been said that we are the only Bible some people will ever read. You may tell people about Jesus, and they may never listen. You may invite them to church, and they may never come. But your life is a constant Gospel message. Do your actions preach a powerful sermon?

Maybe your actions have preached a hypocritical sermon. I'm haunted by all the times mine have. But God offers forgiveness, that we might learn to fear Him. We need His grace more than anything. And it's ours to own, if we'll accept it with a sincere heart. Because Jesus took the punishment our sins deserved, the wrath and justice of the Father have been satisfied. Now we can be blameless in the eyes of a flawless God. And with the power of the Holy Spirit, we can live like it too.

I guess dreams really do come true. I longed for the Great Delete Button. Life doesn't give me that. But Jesus does. I wished I could become a kid and start all over. Life never let me do that. But Jesus says I can be born again.

I thought my scars would never heal. But I touch Jesus' wounds, and now, at last, my own are healed.

Chapter 7

His Body for Our Bodies

I'm pretty sure I'd be the most depressed person in the world if it weren't for Jesus.

How does anyone get through a single day without Him? It just boggles my mind. I mean, how can a human being possibly make sense of life if they think there's no such thing as God? If God weren't in the picture life would make zero sense to me. If there were no God to alleviate my guilt, lift my burdens, and apply balm to my wounds, I think I'd have given up long ago.

But when you discover Jesus, life becomes such a blast. I'm convinced that being a child of God is the greatest thing in the world. The absolute greatest thing. I've been a Christian for twenty years, and I'm telling you, it just keeps getting better. I definitely get why they call this message the Gospel, which means "good news." It's just so . . . good. Why more people don't believe the Gospel is beyond me. I know a few billion people in the world do believe, but for crying out loud, why doesn't everyone just get saved already!

So in light of the breath-taking message of the Gospel that we've been talking about, I want to ask you a very important question . . .

If Jesus gave you His body, are you giving Him your body?

When Jesus died on the cross, God used the blood of His Son as currency to purchase our bodies, which is why the Bible says, "God bought you with a high price. So you must honor God with your body." Christ's body was turned over from God to Satan, to be marred on the cross, so that we could turn our bodies from Satan to God, to be used for purity.

Yet sadly, one of the scariest issues confronting the youth today is the problem of sexual immorality. You can't even walk into a convenience store, go on the Internet, or turn on the TV without it attacking your eyes. All a person has to do is turn on their computer and they're free to explore the wide world of lust. Or have you tried flipping through the channels lately? Good luck. I bet within sixty seconds your eyes will be dirtied up. We live in a culture where every American has at their fingertips the power to indulge in any type of sexual immorality.

It really bums me out because there are so many great movies that had to be ruined by a stupid sex scene. It doesn't make sense why they have to put that in there. I guess it's because we live in a culture where sex sells. Apparently the money mongrels are aware of this too. So they capitalize on it and sell their souls just to make a few more bucks at the box office.

This really bugs me.

Paul, I really agree with you when you told your young friend Timothy, nearly two thousand years ago, to run from anything that stimulates youthful lusts. This is a great ideal, for sure. The only problem is a bunch of people think this command is impossible to obey nowadays. "Let's be realistic," the cynics say. "How can we expect our youth to run away from the temptations? Our culture has provided way too many opportunities for them to dive into lust. It's simply not reasonable to expect them to be 'pure' in *this* day and age."

Tell that to Joseph. He'd have something to say to these skeptics. Maybe you remember his story. As a young man, Joseph was serving in Egypt under a man named Potiphar, who was the captain of the palace guard. Well, Potiphar had a wily wife who had a lusting problem, so when she caught a glimpse of the buff, handsome Hebrew slave called Joseph, she wanted him. She invited him to sleep with her, but he told her there was no way. "Look," he said, "my master trusts me with everything in his entire household. No one here has more authority than I do! He has held nothing back from me except you, because you are his wife. How could I ever do such a wicked thing? It would be a great sin against God."

But she didn't exactly get the hint. Day after day, she kept pressuring him to sleep with her. Day after day he refused. Joseph wisely kept as far away from her as he possibly could.

But this woman didn't take no for an answer. One day, when no one was around, as Joseph was doing work inside the house she snuck in and grabbed him by his cloak, demanding that he sleep with her. But Joseph football juked out of his cloak and sprinted out of the house. Potiphar's wife was left holding his cloak in her hand as he bolted off toward safety. But being the sneaky woman she was, she kept his garment so that when her husband came home that night she had "evidence" that *he* was the one trying to rape *her*. Potiphar was ticked. So he threw Joseph into prison.

You've got to admire the guy. No matter how relentless the seductress was, Joseph just wouldn't budge. "Well that would have been easy for him," one might argue. "Potiphar's wife was probably no temptation at all." I agree that when you read the story it's easy to picture her as, well, sort of a desperate ogre. I mean, how many stories are there of a woman trying to rape a strong man? It seems like she must have waddled toward him like a huge beast and said with a gruff, manly voice, "Lie with me." But I don't think that was the case. Remember, Potiphar was a very important and influential man in Egypt, so I bet he had his choice of women. No doubt he would have chosen a very beautiful bride.

But although his wife was probably an attractive woman, Joseph would not be seduced by her.

Joseph proved the skeptics wrong. He proved that even when the temptations are fierce, there's always a door with an exit sign on it. Like Joseph, we too can disprove the critics. We can show them that purity *is* possible in the twenty-first century, despite the countless seductions swirling around us.

Now, I realize you've probably heard a bunch of messages about purity. You've read books on the topic. Attended purity seminars. Heard statistics about STD's and venereal diseases and teen pregnancies. You're aware of how sex outside of marriage can destroy your body. All of these things are good to know. But in this chapter, that's not what I want to talk to you about. I don't want to talk to you about what lust does to your body, but what it does to your soul, your life, and your future.

I'll never forget the night I heard the best message on purity of all time. A few years back me and a couple buddies started a high school Bible study at my house in Costa Mesa. Well, one night I asked my dad if he would teach. This happened to be the night my future wife Necia was there, because she was visiting from Oregon with her mom who is great friends with my mom. It's pretty crazy what he "happened" to be talking about that night. Purity and relationships. Me and Necia wouldn't start dating until years later when I moved back to Oregon, but we both were present for this eye-opening teaching.

My dad opened up the Word as me and my friends sat on the living room floor. He taught us that guys and girls are like cups. The guys have blue food-dye in their cups, the girls have red food-dye in theirs. When a guy and girl get married and have sex inside of marriage, they pour their cups into each other, back and forth, and the two become one. Now they are no longer red and blue, but their colors are mixed into purple. He talked about how this is a very beautiful thing.

But sex outside of marriage is different. Rather than pouring the two colors into each other to become one color, you are actually dumping the food-dye out of your cups. Each time you have sex outside of marriage, you are spilling a part of your color onto the floor. And you'll never be able to get it back.

He told us that this is how our souls work. When people have sex within marriage, their souls blend beautifully into one. But every time people have sex outside of marriage, a part of their souls gets dumped out. That's why those who are always having sex with all these different people get this glazed look in their eyes. The windows to their soul reveal there's nothing there. They used to look so beautiful, but something's different now. Part of who they once were is gone, their inner beauty fading.

So whenever you hear a guy brag to his buddies, "I got a piece of her!" that's exactly what he did. He got a piece of her soul that she'll never be able to get back. A part of her personality has been spilled on the ground, forever lost. This is the reason, my dad went on to teach, that Proverbs 6:32 says when a person commits adultery they destroy their own soul.

I'd have to say sexual immorality is one of the top five most selfish sins ever. It doesn't just spill your own soul, but also the soul of the person you're sinning with. And on top of that, you're both robbing your future spouses by stealing a piece of each other. So when you get married and long to give your whole self to your spouse, part of you will be missing because you already gave away a piece to your girlfriend/boyfriend.

But notice, when Potiphar's wife tried to seduce Joseph, he didn't say, "How could I rob my future spouse by spilling a part of my soul?" Nor did he say, "How could I steal a piece of your personality from you?" He didn't even say, "How could I betray my master who has given me so much?" No. He said, "How could I do this great sin against *God?*" He knew that sex outside of marriage hurt a lot of people. But he knew it hurt God more than anyone else.

Did you know we can actually hurt God's feelings? The Bible says we can bring sorrow to the Holy Spirit by the way we live. Isn't that terrible? Within our grasp is the dreadful power to break God's heart. In fact, when the Israelites went off to worship their idols, the Lord described them as going "a whoring" after other gods. He felt spiritually cheated on. They were having an affair right in front of Him. This broke His heart.

Your body is the temple of the Holy Ghost, so when you think you're alone with your girlfriend, think again. You bring Jesus with you into every situation you put yourself in. He's inside your body, even as we speak. Where you go, He goes.

So how could we break Jesus' heart by having a spiritual affair before His very eyes? How could we join our bodies to another person (outside of marriage) if God joined His body to the tree to purchase ours? He gave His all for us . . .

Now it's time for us to give *our* all for Him.

Chapter 8

Lust is a Pop Quiz, Not Just an SAT

"But I already blew it!" you may be thinking. "My one chance to abstain from sexual immorality has been squandered. The Purity Ship has sailed . . . so I guess I might as well keep giving in." If you really stop to think about it though, wouldn't you agree that this is pretty much the stupidest logic ever?

Solomon nailed it when he asked, "Can a man scoop fire into his lap and not be burned?" He understood that we humans know lust is going to hurt us really bad, and yet we stubbornly scoop it up for ourselves anyways. So he likens lust to a fire. When you feed it, it burns away part of what makes you you. This you know. But let me ask you this, if you've already burned a piece of yourself, why would you go on and burn the rest? If you've scooped fire into your lap, that really stinks, for sure. But why would you go ahead and scoop it into your mouth and ears while you're at it?

Think of it this way. Imagine you are sitting next to a living room fire. Suddenly, your hand slips and gets thrust into the flames. Your hand gets burned off and you scream because it hurts like crazy. What if right after that happened you said, "Well, I guess because I burnt my hand off, I might as well burn my arm, my shoulder, and half of my face off while I'm at it." You'd be nuts. Obviously you would stop burning yourself so you can save what's left of your body. So too, if you've burned a piece of yourself through lust, stop now while you still have at least some of your soul left over. Sexual immorality may have scarred you, but don't let it scar you any further!

Have you ever asked a kid what he wanted to be when he grew up? I bet you he didn't say, "I want to be a porn addict." Or "I want to be a child molester." Or "I want to be a player and cheat on my wife." No kid says that. But many kids grow up to be these things. Why? At first their lust was just a little spark, but they fanned that spark until *over time* it became a wild fire that destroyed their life. Initially they started out with a little hand burn. But their fire wasn't satisfied, so they kept feeding it. Girls weren't enough, so they had to move on to guys. Then to little kids. The fire spread to the shoulder, then to the face, and before they know it their whole body is aflame in lust. Their gross lifestyle didn't *just happen.* They didn't wake up one morning, look in the bathroom mirror and say, "I think I'm going to be a prostitute" or "a child molester today." Their *every day decisions* made their lust progressive and ultimately destructive.

Always remember, sexual temptation isn't just an SAT, but a pop quiz. It's not simply a one-time test, but an exam that must be taken every day. I used to think the story of Potiphar's wife trying to rape Joseph was Joseph's One Big Test. If he passed, he graduated as a man of God. If he failed, he flunked out and was a loser at life. But it struck me that the Bible says she put pressure on him *day by day.* He had to be tested by lust's "pop quizzes" on a daily basis, and that prepared him for the *big* test, the SAT so to speak, when she flung herself at him in the empty house. But because he aced the everyday quizzes, he was ready for the SAT.

Many good teachers give their students regular pop quizzes to prepare them for the one time SAT at the end of the year. SAT's are huge, I mean they help determine the rest of your life, whether or not you get into college. The teacher knows if his students can pass the many little exams, they'll be ready for the big test at the end of the year.

Joseph was not overwhelmed by the big test because he had been given small quizzes along the way. This is really cool to think about, but God can actually turn the temptations the demons send our way into training for the really intense trials. Because of this training, the Bible promises you'll never encounter a temptation that's too hot for you to handle. You'll be ready for it because God has already taught you how to take the Way of Escape. He knows just how many quizzes you'll need to take in order to ace the SAT's.

Lust is a battle that must be fought every single day. Jesus said if you want to follow Him, you must pick up your cross *daily*. Picking up your cross is not a one time thing, but a decision you make every morning when you're alarm clock goes off. You've got to make the deliberate choice to crucify your sinful nature with each sunrise. But remember, Jesus didn't say, "If you want to follow Me, pick up your dandelion daily and let's frolic in the hills together." Nor did He say, "If you want to follow Me, pick up your Diet Coke daily and let's soak in the sun together." He said, "If You want to follow Me, pick up Your *cross* daily and let's get crucified together."

That's not an easy challenge. But Jesus never said it would be easy. He warned us that crucifying our sinful nature on a daily basis is bloody business. It's hard. But just as a seed cannot grow unless it dies and is buried in the ground, so we cannot grow as people unless we first bury our sinful nature.

But you might be saying to yourself, "I don't need to read on. I've got this purity thing covered! I haven't given in to temptation in five years!" Or maybe you're saying "It's been five hours since I last messed up. I'm doing pretty decent, if I do say so myself. Don't need to hear any more about purity. But I definitely know *someone else* who does!" If that's you, all I have to say is good luck. Satan's got your number. The Bible warns people who think they stand to watch out, lest they fall down. Their pride goes before a fall, and temptation hits them like Ray Lewis from the blind side.

The best time to prepare for the battle of lust is during the seasons you aren't struggling with it. Remember the story of King Asa? For the first decade of his reign his land had total peace. But at the ten year mark, a *massive* attack came his way. A million Ethiopians declared war on the land of Judah. That's a lot of people. In *Two Towers*, for example, in the sweet battle at Helm's Deep, there are about ten thousand Uruk-Hai who do battle against the men of Rohan. There's a ton of them. But can you imagine *one million* fierce warriors waging war on you? That'd be a fairly terrifying introduction to warfare. But King Asa was ready for them. Why? Because during his ten years of peace he wasn't slurping lemonade, eating grapes, and having servants fan him with palm tree branches. He didn't say, "We got peace man! Let's just relax." No. He was hard at work building up the fortified cities to make the land ready for a war. Because he was preparing for battle in an era of peace, he was ready when the attack came.

You may not be battling lust at the moment. The demon archers may not be flinging fiery darts of temptation at you now. But get ready. A spiritual battle is coming. Are you preparing for it? Are you seeking God in times of peace, or do you just call out when the Enemy is at your doorstep? By then it may be too late. Pass the daily pop quizzes, carry the daily cross, have your daily hang out sesh with the Lord. And when the SAT's come around, when the Ethiopian army declares war, when Potiphar's wife flings herself at you, you'll be ready. So can I challenge you to do something? This really will work. Beg the Lord, every single day, to guard you against sexual immorality. But if you think you don't need to, if you think you stand, take heed lest you fall on the field of battle. Call for aid. Build up the fortified cities. Summon the troops.

The Enemy's coming.

Chapter 9

Cassandra and Jamal

Can I just say something that makes absolutely no sense to me? When people ask, "How far can I go physically with my girlfriend before it's a sin?" As C.S. Lewis would say, that's like asking what shape is yellow. The question doesn't make sense. What people are really asking when they bring up this question is, "How close can I get to the line of sin without actually crossing it?" The question shouldn't be how close can you get to the line of sin, but how *far away* can you run from it.

That's why Paul told Timothy to "flee youthful lusts." He didn't tell him to flirt with youthful lusts, or entertain youthful lusts, but run in the polar opposite direction! When Joseph was grabbed by Potiphar's wife, he ran away. Joseph didn't say to her, "Well we can hug . . . that's not all that bad." He didn't greet her with a "holy kiss." He didn't think, "I don't want to hurt her feelings by making a break for it, so maybe I can just meet her at Starbucks tomorrow morning at nine and explain why I can't do bad stuff with her." No. Joseph split. It didn't matter that it hurt her feelings. He did what he had to do.

I'm telling you the truth, if you don't run like the wind from things that stimulate youthful lusts, if you just hang out around the line of sin, eventually you're going to cross it. It's just going to happen. When you push your luck, tip-toeing the line of lust with the girl you're dating, the movies you're watching, or the sites you're browsing, you will end up stepping over it. This happens all the time.

Ask Jamal and Cassandra, the dating couple I just made up (at first I used the names Matt and Sarah, but if they're made up why not give them exotic names). Jamal says to Cassandra, "We'll just hug for a sec, but we'll never do the bad stuff!" Cassandra agrees. But when a fleeting moment of temptation comes, because they're already in a hugging position, they just can't resist. Like a magnet they're drawn over their boundary line. And so they give in "just this once."

But everyone knows it never really is "just this once." Once a couple says yes to temptation, even if it's just once, it becomes *a lot* harder to say no the next time. They already got a sample of the forbidden fruit. Now they know what it tastes like . . . so they need another bite. Pandora's Box has been opened. They got a foot in the door, and now lust will rush into their lives like a savage flood.

Jamal and Cassandra learn this the hard way.

At first they feel really bad about what they've done, but a few days later they find they've got themselves into another tempting spot. This time Cassandra says to Jamal. "Well we've already said yes once . . . what's the point of saying no now? We might as well do it again." Jamal finds this rather logical. *After all, why not? Might as well do a second time what we've done a first.* So they cross the line once more.

They feel bad again. But not quite as bad as the first time. The first time they were scandalized, but now the initial shock factor isn't there. So when the next day rolls around, so does another temptation. They're surprised to discover that it's become far easier to say yes to their passions this time than it was the first two times. So Cassandra and Jamal mess up and cross Boundary Line Number Three.

Now Jamal says something very dangerous.

"Yeah we messed up," he casually remarks, "but at least we're not doing what Orlando and Sophia are doing. They do way worse stuff than us." And as they begin to compare their sin with Orlando and Sophia's "bigger" sins, they begin to feel much better about themselves.

They feel this newfound comparison gives them liberty to push their boundary line back a little bit further. They figure it's okay as long as they're "not quite as bad" as Orlando and Sophia.

"There's no way we'll cross the line now that it's this far back!" says Cassandra. "We'll never cross it now," agrees Jamal. "We may have done *this*, but we'll certainly never do *that*." So they tip-toe the line once more. But later that night, when they're alone after a date, a wave of weakness comes over Jamal. And because he's put himself in an enticing situation yet again, he convinces Cassandra to step over the boundary line just one more time. They fall again.

Pause for a minute. Don't you think it's interesting Jesus didn't teach us to pray, "Lead us not into sin," but rather, "Lead us not into temptation." It's as if He understood how weak we humans really are. Just lead us to a place of temptation, and it's pretty much guaranteed we're going to sin. Lead us away from the places that make us feel tempted, and we don't sin. Pretty simple concept. I wonder how drastically our lives would change if we didn't focus so much on "not sinning" as much as simply staying away from situations that will even *tempt* us.

Well, back to Cassandra and Jamal. They're pretty down on themselves at this point. They can't believe they crossed their boundary line even after they pushed it back. But because they won't flee the places that weaken them, they keep falling. A fifth time. A sixth. But by about the seventh time, their guilt begins to wear off.

"We may be doing what Orlando and Sophia are doing now," Jamal says to Cassandra. "But did you hear about how far Treyson and Georgina went last week?" And so Jamal and Cassandra justify themselves through comparison once more. Their quest toward disaster is underway.

Did you know the Bible says you can actually sear your conscience as with a hot iron? A good way to do this is to copy Jamal and Cassandra. They broke their moral compass, their inner gauge of right and wrong, because they kept on sinning and comparing.

You know, if you shut the door on the Holy Spirit enough times He's not going to knock any more. He won't keep ringing the doorbell if no one answers. If He keeps convicting you, but you don't open the door of your heart for Him, eventually He will stop. That's why some people can literally sleep around every night and not even feel bad. You know what people I'm talking about? The first time they crossed their boundary line they felt horrible, like they were the worst sinners ever. But over time sexual immorality became a habit, and each time they said "yes" to temptation their conscience became a little more desensitized. Before they know it their conscience is completely numbed. Their "spiritual nerves" aren't working any more. Lust is burning them alive, and they don't even realize it! Isn't that terrifying?

That's why creaking open the door of lust is such a scary thing. Give the Devil one single "yes", and it becomes harder and harder to say no the next time. Lust has a domino effect. That's why every temptation is *so* important, because it starts small, but feed it once and it'll spread rapidly. As Gandalf the White would say it's "like the falling of small stones that starts an avalanche."

The reciprocal is also true, say "no" to the Devil just once, and it will become easier and easier to resist him, and eventually he will flee. Both the Devil and the Spirit are knocking on your heart, which one are you inviting in?

Someone's got to flee, but it's up to you which one you submit to and which one you resist.

This is why I need to tell you what I think is one of the worst sins out there. This might offend you. I really don't mean to be offensive. But I really believe this, so I'm going to say it.

First, I want to talk to you if you're a girl reading this. 1 Timothy 2:9 teaches that women should dress modestly. Why does Paul say this? Is he a strict Christian schoolteacher who is trying to bog you down with rules? Is he telling you this because he doesn't want you to have any fun, dress cool, or enjoy fashion? Does he just think Amish clothes are the only ones Christians can wear? No. I think Paul said this because he understood what's really going on when you dress immodestly. When you're walking around with scandalous clothes on, *everywhere* you go you're awakening lust in the men around you. Hebrews 10:24 says, "provoke one another to good works," but when you dress immodestly, you're provoking men to *evil* works (maybe that's why they call scandalous clothes "provocative"). This is why I think immodest dressing is one of the deadliest sins young women can fall into. Think about it: when you put sketchy clothes on, you are deliberately inviting every man who will see you that day to indulge in lust. Obviously that may not be your intention. But it is your reality. Wherever you happen to go that day, to church, to school, or to the store, you are inspiring guy after guy after guy to lust after you.

This would be a scary thing to answer to God for. Could you imagine Him saying, "I asked you to wear modest clothes, but because you didn't, you caused 858,992 men to sin in your lifetime." It doesn't just affect you, but everyone you happen to walk by that day.

You know what else is scary about dressing immodestly? Let's say you're at Dairy Queen one day waiting in line. There's a guy standing next to you, and the way you're dressed incites fleshly desire in him. So he goes home, with lust in his mind, and looks at pornography for the first time. And because he says "yes" once, the progressive lust begins to take over and he becomes a porn addict, all because you opened the door for him. I know that may sound ridiculous or way out there, but scandalous clothes can really do this. Like yeast, lust starts small but spreads rapidly. Never forget that you have the power to provoke men to the basest forms of evil simply by the way you dress.

But I think the Enemy lies to a lot of girls by telling them there are no cool clothes that are also modest. In my opinion (which I know doesn't count for much, especially as a guy) some of the coolest fashion designers make "appropriate" clothes. I know clothes are important to 99% of American girls, but whatever style you like, you *can* wear your fashion modestly. You don't have to wear a middle-eastern robe and veil to dress decently you know.

You want to know another effective piece of fiction the Devil uses on girls? He tells them that they are beautiful only if they can get men to desire them sexually. Trust me, the guys who look at you in an immoral way are not the kind of guys you want to be with. They're shallow guys looking for shallow girls. These are not the kind of guys who care about you. They simply take what they want, get tired of it real quick, and then move on to someone else. So does it really make much sense to awaken temporary desire in a guy you'll never want to be with?

Now before I close this chapter let me talk to you guys for a second. I know it may seem crazy, but the Bible promises you will never actually be tempted above what you're able to handle. There will always, *always* be a way of escape. Joseph could've said (as many guys say), "*She* came on to *me*, man. She grabbed my coat for crying out loud . . . I couldn't do anything about it!" Joseph didn't fall back on this overly-used excuse. He saw a tiny window of escape, and he took it. He had a five second opportunity to juke out of her reach, and that's exactly what he did.

You may be convinced that you're addicted to lust. That there's no way to beat it. It's got you by the coat, and you can't disobey its demands. But God says this isn't true. Next time you're tempted, there *will* be a window of escape. Granted, that window may only be a five second window. But it'll be there. So take it, right away. Like Joseph, see just how fast you can run away from the Seductress. If that means literally running out of the house, taking an ice-cold shower, or calling a friend, do whatever it takes. The escape *will* be there. Just don't take the girl to Starbucks, if you know what I mean. Don't entertain the thought. Don't hug for "only a few more minutes." Simply run as fast as you can.

A few years ago I was at a high school retreat. My friend Andy was teaching, and he talked to the guys about purity. There was something he said that I still remember to this day. He said if you need to break your computer, then break your computer. Wise piece of advise.

You don't need Facebook as bad as you think.

Chapter 10

A Dungeon of Dreamers

The truth is, if you choose to be pure you're going to suffer. It's just inevitable. I'd like to tell you, "Hey, if you're pure, everything is going to be hunky dory and everyone will like you and things will get much easier!"

But that's just not the case.

The Bible says if you want to live godly in Christ Jesus you *will* suffer persecution. Not might. But will. When you tell people you're saving yourself for marriage, your friends may make fun of you, you might not get invited to the parties, and your boyfriend may break up with you because you won't go any further with him.

But when you're unjustly sitting in your lonely social prison cell, remember the same thing happened to Joseph. Because he refused to do bad stuff with Potiphar's wife, she had him thrown into a dungeon. The same thing is going to happen to you. Choose to be pure, and you're going to get hurt. I know that's not a big selling point . . .

But check this out. Purity will lead you to suffering, *but suffering will lead you to your dreams.*

So who just so happened to be in the same dungeon Joseph was in? The cupbearer of Pharaoh himself. Pharaoh got ticked at him for some reason, but when his wrath subsided he released him and gave him his job back. Well Pharaoh just so happened to have some troubling dreams one night, but no one could tell him what they meant. The cupbearer remembered Joseph's unique ability to interpret dreams, so Pharaoh called him up right away. Joseph revealed the meaning of the dreams, and because of this, Pharaoh made him Prime Minister of Egypt, the second most powerful man in all the land, a fulfillment of Joseph's own dreams he had thirteen years earlier! How cool is that?

If Joseph wouldn't have stood for purity, he wouldn't have been sent to prison. But if he wouldn't have been sent to prison, he wouldn't have met the cupbearer. And if he hadn't met the cupbearer, he would've never met Pharaoh. And had he never met Pharaoh, he would've never been lifted up to his dreams.

Isn't that crazy? God was orchestrating Joseph's life like a Master Conductor. His dreams came to pass all because he chose to stand up for purity. Was Joseph's plot dark? Yes. Did purity lead him to suffering? Yes. But the suffering is what led him to his dreams.

I know being pure isn't going to be easy. Especially in this wicked and perverse generation in which we live. People will mock you. You'll feel like you're all alone sometimes. You may get thrown into the social dungeon. But the dungeon is the pathway to your dreams.

So let's be dungeon dreamers together.

Let's copy Joseph's example and give our bodies to God. This is our destiny. But I have to admit I think it's kind of funny when I say we should "give God our bodies" because how can we give Him what He already possesses? We've already stated that Jesus bought our bodies from us with the currency of His blood, so that means our bodies are rightfully His.

I have this habit of offering people stuff that isn't mine. Like this last Wednesday night. I was sitting in Bible study and I needed a pen. Necia reached in her purse and handed me this really cool pen made of recycled materials (like popsicle sticks or something). I generously told her, "Take this pen whenever you need it," as if I were being polite to give her permission to use *her* pen.

Or sometimes when I visit my family's house I offer guests food from the cabinet. "Take a Fresca! You want me to grab you some grapes from the fridge? And there's Doritos in the cabinet." But I sometimes forget that it's not my house. I'm "graciously" offering food that isn't mine and feel like a pretty nice guy while I'm doing it.

The truth is, it's not all that generous to give our bodies to God. It's just our "reasonable service." By "giving" Him our bodies what we're really doing is acknowledging that they're His possession to begin with. When we think we're awesome for giving Him our bodies, it's like we're sneaking into the heavenly Father's garage, finding an old dusty book He hasn't read in a long time, and giving it to Him for Father's Day, hoping He will forget it belonged to Him in the first place.

Your body is rightfully His. So don't get upset when you suffer for being pure, and don't be frustrated if you feel God's under-appreciating you. He's not. Our caring Father isn't commanding you to refrain from sexual pleasure because He's mean and wants you to suffer. Just the opposite. He knows that the suffering you endure, because you've chosen purity, is simply the road to your dreams.

If however, like me, there are many mistakes you've made and things you desperately wish you'd done differently, read chapter 6 again. Go back to the cross, press the Great Delete Button with fear and trembling, and start afresh. Fall at the feet of Jesus and listen to Him tell you, "I do not condemn you. Go your way and sin no more." *There is forgiveness with Him, that He might be feared.* Embark now on the pathway of purity, and the last page of your story will read ...

And so they lived happily ever after.

Chapter 11

If Not Now, When?

Ferocious challenges and breath-taking hopes. We need them both. So far, the majority of this book has been dealing with the challenges. I've thrown down the gauntlet in attempt to summon us to holiness. But now, for the next part of this book, I want to dive into some of the fantastical hope of the Bible.

So I'm stoked to talk to you about one of my of my all-time favorite Biblical subjects, the subject of dreaming big for God. As Joseph discovered, God's dreams for him were bigger than his own were for himself. The beautiful thing is that this is true for our lives too.

The funniest thing happened to me last week. I was supposed to meet with my friend Isaiah at Taco Bell at 12, but I was running a little late. I live right next to Taco Bell, and I figured it'd only take me two seconds to get there. But when I got into the parking lot, the traffic was crazy. I felt like I was on an LA freeway at 5 PM on a weekday. I think it was so crazy because there was a bunch of construction going on (and because Taco Bell is the most de-lish restaurant ever so of course a lot of traffic would go there). But it was weirdly packed out and I got stuck behind a long line of cars in the parking lot. I could see the building to my left, but I was trapped in this traffic line. I was seriously waiting there forever as I became more and more late. Finally, the second car in line decided to wait no longer, so it pulled out from the line and went its own way. The next car followed and then the next. But the first car was still waiting there. When I finally pulled out and passed the first car, I noticed the reason the car wasn't going anywhere. No one was in the drivers seat. We were all waiting in traffic behind a car that had no one in it! Because of the construction the parking lot was set up differently and this guy just decided to park in the lane.

I was going nowhere fast because I was following a parked car. And the truth is, a lot of people don't go anywhere in life because they're following the people around them who have no clue what they're doing with their lives. Many people are in park, and too often we follow them. But it's time to pull out, and you'll be surprised how others will follow you.

A lot of times we say we're waiting for God when in reality He is the One waiting for us. He's given us the green lights, but we're in park and everyone around us is honking wondering why we're not going anywhere. I've noticed a trend in a lot of people my age is that they claim the phrase, "I'm waiting on God" when in reality they're just eating Doritos and playing Xbox.

That is not waiting on God.

As I mentioned earlier, I have this terrible tendency to procrastinate. I may call my procrastination "waiting on God" but in reality I'm just being lazy or I'm too afraid to actually take a leap of faith. Like you, I believe God has planted dreams inside me, but too often I think I have more time to pursue them than I really do. I say to myself, "I will go for my dreams for sure . . . when I have more time." But the funny thing about that statement is that I will not have any more time tomorrow than I have today. It's not like I'll get 26 hours in my day when I turn 30 as opposed to 24 hours a day now.

That's why my all-time favorite quote, my life quote, was uttered by Hillel the Elder when he said, "If not now, when?" I get insanely inspired every time I think about this quote, so much so I wrote it on my bookmarker and put it in my *Lord of the Rings* book. Every time I look at it I know I've got to get moving.

If I'm not going big for Jesus now, and chasing the dreams He's given me, then when will I?

So let me ask you a very difficult question . . .

What are you doing with your life?

Can I encourage you to set this book down for just a second to ponder this? The problem is, most the time when we're confronted with this question we opt for the TV clicker and say, "I'll think about that later." Or we pick up our cell phone to send off a text or log onto Facebook because we haven't checked up on it in a total of thirty eternal minutes!

The truth is, when I'm faced with the all-important question, "What are you doing with your life, Ben?" I think of my life in huge terms: what have I done over the past few years? What do I plan to do in the next decade? That's fine. But the question is really simpler than I make it. The reality is that life is not made up of the tomorrows or the yesterdays but of the todays. So I want you and me to re-phrase the question from "what am I doing with my life?" to "what am I doing with my *today?*" Because what I am doing with my today determines what I am doing with my life.

You've heard the saying, "tomorrow never comes." If you think about it, it's amazing how true that is. As I'm typing right now, the date is June 19th, 2010. June 19th is today. But yesterday, on June 18th, June 19th was my tomorrow. When I woke up this morning, however, I didn't stretch my arms and say, "June 19th is here! At last I've reached my tomorrow!" No. June 19th is just another today. Tomorrow never actually comes. As the quote goes, "today is the tomorrow you were waiting for yesterday."

So if not now, when? Are you the person you dreamed of being five years ago? Are you any closer to your dreams right now than you were last week?

Maybe you're saying, "I'll pursue my dreams later." But you said that a year ago. *Today* is the tomorrow you waited for yesterday. And before you know it, today will be another yesterday you can never get back.

I think we'd be wise to heed the words of Oogway the Turtle when he told Kung Fu Panda, "Yesterday is history, tomorrow is a mystery, but today is a gift . . . that is why it is called the present." Today is one of the greatest presents you've been given. But you only have 24 hours to open it.

In James 4:14, the apostle said, "For your life is like the morning fog - it's here a little while then it's gone." This is one of the most accurate descriptions of life I've ever heard. When I was in jr. high, my parents used to drive us kids down to Newport Beach for vacation. I was so excited about getting some sunny Southern Californian weather, but I remember feeling kind of bummed out when I would wake up in the morning because I'd look out the window only to see overcast weather. I'd seen enough clouds in Oregon, you know? It was time for some sun! But the craziest thing would happen (if you've been to Newport you'll know what I'm talking about). What I thought was overcast weather was really just a morning fog, and a few hours into the day it would disappear completely. Just like that! It was there . . . and then I'd pretty much turn my head and it'd be gone. So I got to enjoy bright blue skies and the rays of sun on my face after all. And although it looked like the thick morning fog was there to stay, it just wanted to hang out on the beach for a couple hours. That's all. And it was gone before I knew it.

James says our lives are like that. From all appearances it looks like we're here to stay, but we're not. We're a morning fog, and we'll be gone before we know it. Just yesterday I got a text message from my sister that said our friend's fiancé went home to be with the Lord. That's crazy. Yesterday a 29-year-old soul was taken to Heaven. Like a morning fog, his life evaporated suddenly and unexpectedly . . . just like that.

Please hear me on this. I know because we're young we think we're immortal. But we're not. We're going to die before we know it. And I'm telling you, the more we think about death the more fully we will live our lives. The more we understand the shortness of life the less we will waste our time. I'm already shocked at how quickly I'm racing to the grave. Just yesterday I was in 6th grade, playing capture the flag at Jacksonville Elementary. Now I'm twenty-two. Crazy. But you know what people who are older than me tell me? "Ben, you think life is going by fast *now* . . . well just you wait. You haven't seen nothin' yet." I guess the saying is true that life is like a toilet paper roll, the closer you get to the end the faster it goes.

That's why, personally, one my biggest prayers for this year of my life is that it would go by slower than any other year I've lived. I only have 365 days in this year, and not many years after that. It's 10:25 AM, but before I know it, it will be 10:25 PM, and as I lay my head on the pillow tonight, another today is gone.

The best way to let your life pass you by is to let today pass you by. So pin the date up to the wall, and don't let it go until you've had your way with it . . .

If not now, when?

Chapter 12

God's Promises are Not for Window Shoppers

I don't get window shopping. It's just not logical. If you're a guy you understand me . . .

So you go into a store, find a jacket you really like and say to yourself, "Wow that's a cool jacket! Too bad I can't buy it." Then you go to the next store and say, "Wow those are cool jeans. Wish they were mine." You go to the next store and think, "If only I could have that dress! Bummer I got those bills coming up." So at the end of your shopping day you look at a bunch of clothes but have no actual shopping bags in your hands. It seems like torture. Window shopping's kind of like going to Food 4 Less with no cash and looking at a bunch of bananas and Cheerios boxes for the sake of looking at a bunch of bananas and Cheerios boxes. I don't know, it just seems kind of depressing to me.

If you're a girl I'm sure you like to window shop, so I mean no offense. If that's your thing, more power to you. Necia loves it too. It's just a natural girl instinct I suppose. But you know what's funny? As unreasonable as it seems to me as a guy, I window shop for the promises of God all the time.

For example, I'll be having devotions and read Matthew 7:7 which says, "ask and you will receive." I look at it and think, "Wow what a pretty promise." But then when I pray that day I don't have all that much faith. Why? Because I looked at the promise and admired it, but I walk away without actually owning it. Or I read Philippians 4:13 which says, "I can do all things through Christ who strengthens me." I pump my fist and declare, "Yeah! I can do *anything* with

Jesus!" But then when I have a hard day I complain to my wife and say, "I'm not going to make it Neesh!"

Maybe you do the same thing. Maybe you're window shopping even as we speak. You underlined Philippians 4:19 which says God will supply all your needs, but right now you're sweating and panicking because you don't know how you're going to pay rent this month. You don't *really* believe the promise belongs to you.

Like a window shopper who moves from store to store, all too often we move from promise to promise, but never actually own any of them. But God's promises are not for window shoppers. He did not give them to us so we could look at them through a glass window and wish they belonged to us. No. They're not for looking at but for *owning* and *using*. So why not purchase them with Jesus' name and have them for our everyday use, for crying out loud?

Beth Moore wrote a great book called *Believing God* wherein she talked about the necessity of taking God at His Word. In it she discussed the difference between believing *in* God and believing God. All of us Christians believe *in* God, but how many of us really believe God? "Well what's the difference?" you wonder. I'm glad you asked!

Let's say I was an amazing singer (although I can't sing for the life of me in reality), and one day you happen to hear me sing a song. You're amazed. You look me in the eye and tell me you think my future is bright. You tell me you believe in me. So I decide to go out and try for a record deal, and happen to land one only a few weeks later. I dial your number as fast as I can and tell you the wonderful news. But you say, "No way! I don't believe you. How could you possibly get a record deal so fast?" I'd say back to you, "But only two weeks ago you said that you believe *in* me. So why don't you *believe me* when I tell you the great news?"

That's how we treat God sometimes. "I believe in You, God," we declare. But then He gives us awesome news in the Bible, crazy promises, and all too often we say, "I don't believe You ... that promise is just too good to be true." But real giants of faith don't just believe in God, they believe God too. They don't just admire His promises and leave them on the pages of the Bible, but they take them off the page and use them as every day necessities.

Listen to this crazy promise (it's my life-verse by the way): Psalm 37:4 says, "Take delight in the LORD, and He will give you your heart's desires." Isn't that amazing? Many people don't believe God for this promise because they think there's just no way this could be real. I mean, you'd think God would say, "If you weep twice a day over the wickedness of the world," or "If you give *x* amount of money to the poor each week," or "If you don't mess up ... then I'll give you your heart's desires." But that's not what He says. He simply says, "Have a blast with Me and I'll give you your heart's desires." I know it sounds too good to be true. But because God's in it (as the saying goes) *it's so good it's got to be true!*

Last summer I was traveling to our church camp on the coast with my friends Luke and Dave. We stopped at McDonald's off the 5 freeway to grab some lunch (because there was no Taco Bell nearby). I ordered Chicken McNuggets and a small drink. But the craziest thing happened. The guy behind the counter told me it'd be cheaper to buy the big drink. It would literally cost me *more* money to buy the small drink. No joke. I didn't understand why this was so, but I sure accepted it with open arms! I didn't say to the guy, "That's too good to be true man. What's the catch?" No. I just said, "Okay sweet. Give me the big drink!"

When I read a promise like Psalm 37:4, I can tend to think there's a catch. But there's not. It really is that good. No strings attached. When you walk with God and put Him first in your life, He will take your heart and remake it into a mirror that reflects the plans He already has for your life. He molds your desires into puzzle pieces that fit perfectly into His will. Don't ask God what the catch is. Just say, "Sweet! I'll take You at Your Word."

One of the best definitions of Psalm 37:4 I've ever heard was given by Dustin Ruth. Dustin Ruth is the lead singer of Ruth, one of my all-time favorite bands. Their first CD was entitled *Secondhand Dreaming*, and he based this title off of Psalm 37:4. His explanation was so cool . . .

So you know when you're around a smoker? You may have never smoked in your life, but when you're simply in the same atmosphere of a smoker you're going to breathe in the smoke from his cigarette. As you know, this is called "secondhand smoking." The same concept is true when you walk with God. God's dreaming up all these dreams for your life, and when you're simply around Him, you start dreaming them too. If you follow Him around, you'll catch on to His dreams and *His* desires will be on *your* heart. The closer you get to the smoker the more you'll breathe in his smoke. The closer you get to God, the more your heart will breathe in His desires. Secondhand dreaming. Isn't that cool?

When you're walking with God your desires begin to change. You start to want new things. Better things. "Where did that random dream come from?" you wonder. It came straight from Him. You're just dreaming the dreams He's already dreamt up for your life. And of course God would work this way. He chooses to lead us by our desires, not by our hates. He's our Father, and dads always want to bless their kids. If I ask my dad for bread, he doesn't give me a rock to swallow. If I ask for fish for dinner, he doesn't unleash a serpent on me or put a scorpion on my plate. And if our dads want to bless us, how much more our heavenly Father!

In Romans 8:32 Paul asks, "Since God did not spare even His own Son but gave Him up for us all, won't God, who gave us Christ, also give us everything else?" Yes Paul, I believe He will. So I say we dream big for God. I say we follow Jesus around all the time and become secondhand dreamers. I say we take His promises at face value. And I say we don't just look at them through a window, but go in and take them. Can I get an amen?

Chapter 13

You May Have Sunk . . . But At Least You Walked On Water

When I was a kid I used to want to play pro sports. I wanted to be a pro baseball player, basketball player, and football player, then become a pastor after I retired. Kind of like Reggie White. When I got a little older though I just wanted to stick with pro basketball. Sure, it was a far-fetched dream, but I was really passionate about it. Until I turned fifteen. That was when it all changed. I'll never forget that monumental day . . .

I walked into 24 Hour Fitness, looking forward to playing some hoops. I watched the guys run up and down the court, sweaty and passionate about the game. But as I watched a little more closely, something struck me. These guys were probably in their forties, but the way they played gave the impression that they were trying to make the 24 Hour Fitness Hall of Fame or something. It seemed like they were still trying to make the pros. They were calling fouls and yelling at each other, and it didn't seem like anyone was having any fun. Basketball seemed to be these guys' life, and their overly competitive zeal made me feel kind of sad for them.

Right then I caught a glimpse of my future. *That's going to be you, Ben, when you're forty years old,* I thought to myself, *calling fouls on guys at 24 Hour Fitness and still trying to make the pros.* I was terrified as I saw an older Ben running up and down the court sweaty and intense and still trying to "make it."

Suddenly I didn't want to play pro sports anymore.

Now I don't mean to knock the guys playing that day. Not at all. It was just eye-opening for me to realize that life really is bigger than putting a rubber ball through an iron circle. I knew that in my head, but finally it sunk into my heart. After that experience as a fifteen-year-old, basketball didn't seem so important to me. Slowly but surely it lost its attractiveness in my eyes. Don't get me wrong, I still love the game and have a blast playing (I'm about to play with some friends in a couple hours here at church) but it didn't seem like something worth living for anymore, you know?

So while the craving for basketball was being removed from my heart, the Lord began to plant a new desire in me. I suddenly grew this fresh passion to start teaching God's message to my peers. My dreams began to change from wanting to become a pro athlete to wanting to be a Bible teacher. The beginnings of a secondhand dream were being birthed. So my sophomore year me and a couple friends started a Bible study at my house, and let me tell you, it was one of the funnest things I'd ever done. It was even more exciting to me than basketball, and believe me, that's saying a lot.

A year and a half later I began teaching at small youth groups and events, then when I was a senior in high school I joined my dad and brother to become a pastor here at Applegate . . . and now I get to do what I'm crazy about.

My heart breathed in a new dream for my life, and it became a reality. It's honestly crazy to see how every desire that the Lord has kept in my heart has come to pass thus far in my life. I may not have the calling to be a Tim Tebow or Reggie White, but what I'm doing now is a fulfillment of even deeper passions than sports. It's like the Lord knew what I wanted even before I knew I wanted it, so He protected me from second best (basketball) to give me what I really was craving.

I'm telling you, as you have a blast walking with the Lord He will let you borrow the dreams He has for your life, and He will make them all happen, because they belong to Him in the first place! Because of this crazy hope, we would be wise to do what William Carey told us to do: "Expect great things from God, attempt great things for God." We might as well. After all, why not? We've got the assurance of Psalm 37:4. And that is just *one* promise. We have thousands in Scripture! So since we've got all these promises at our disposal, why not take them off the pages of the Bible and *live our lives as though they will actually happen?*

Peter the Apostle was able to attempt great things for God and expect great things from God because he was a secondhand dreamer. Remember his story? Remember when he and his friends were rowing their boat one night when a wild storm came from out of nowhere? It was so violent it looked like they weren't going to make it. But in the nick of time, Jesus came walking on the waves to rescue them. When Peter saw Jesus, he said the craziest thing, "Lord, if it's really You, tell me to come to You by walking on water." Jesus told him to come. So that's what Peter did. He came . . . and he did the impossible.

You know what really hit me about this story? Jesus didn't invite Peter to walk on the water. Peter invited himself. *He* was the one who came up with the crazy idea. He wasn't waiting for some invitation to do something great, rather he took the initiative and barged in on Jesus' miracle! Peter thought, "If Jesus is doing it, then why don't I join Him?" God plopped the desire in Peter's heart, and once he received this secondhand dream he did something about it!

The reason I find this significant is because I've noticed a lot of youth sit in the boat of complacency and wait for Jesus to give them a great idea. I'm prone to this all the time. We ask the Lord, "So, what are You planning to do with my life?" And you know what I think His response is sometimes? "I don't know. What are *you* planning to do with your life?" It's as if He is the One waiting for *us* to take the initiative, be creative, and dream up some crazy ideas for Him.

Maybe it's time to get off the LoveSac and put down the TV clicker in the name of "waiting on God." *He's* waiting for *you,* for crying out loud!

Now don't get me wrong. I realize we are commanded to wait on the Lord 106 times in Scripture. But if you're in a season of waiting, are you doing it proactively or lazily? There's a big difference between twiddling your thumbs and using your waiting time as training. And there's a big difference between "waiting" because you're too afraid to take risks and waiting because God has genuinely given a red light. So let me ask you this. If you are waiting because there's a red light, what are you doing to redeem the time? And if God hasn't given you a red light, why aren't you moving?

If there's a secondhand dream in your heart, give it a chance to become a reality. Take a risk. Step out on a promise. Remember, all Jesus said to Peter was "come," and that one Word gave him power. I know the water of His Word may seem scary to walk on, but it'll prove to be as firm as concrete *once you step out on it.*

"But Ben," you say, "what if I'm wrong? What if I step out and try something great but fail?" Believe me, you *will* fail. Make no mistake about it. It's just going to happen. Nothing great has ever been accomplished without failure along the way (besides Jesus, of course).

I only mentioned the first part of Peter's story. It's true he walked on water with Jesus for a little bit, but the story didn't end there. As he was walking on the sea, he suddenly caught a glimpse of the huge waves around him. He got scared and took his eyes off the Lord, and then he sunk.

Peter did walk on water, but don't forget he sunk too. Now I could be all critical of Peter and say, "Wow, what a failure. He sunk because he doubted the Lord." But you know what Peter could say back to me? "Remember when you were a kid and tried to walk on your swimming pool? Were you able to do it? I didn't think so. I may have sunk . . . but at least I walked on water." It's true. I've sunk every time I tried to walk on the water of my safe swimming pool, yet Peter was able to walk on the water *in the middle of a life-threatening storm.* I didn't risk anything in my attempts, but Peter risked *everything* in his.

See, all through Peter's life he had great victories, but he had great failures too. One minute he tells Jesus He's the Christ, and the Lord calls Peter a rock. But the next minute he tries to stop Jesus from being crucified, and Jesus called him Satan. One minute he tells the Lord that he wants to die with Him, the next minute he denies Jesus because he was pressured by a little girl. One minute he's running away from Jesus' cross, the next minute he asks to be crucified upside down for his Lord. One minute he uses a sword to chop off a guy's ear, the next minute he uses the Sword of the Spirit to save 3,000 people. One minute he's walking on water, the next minute he's sinking. My point is that whenever you try great things you will also have great failures.

But here's the thing. Each time Peter made a mistake he learned from it. His failures taught him how to succeed. *Each mistake he learned from was a step toward victory.*

As you know, Thomas Edison failed tons of times when he tried to perfect the light bulb. But he said, "I haven't failed, I've found 10,000 ways that don't work." Each time we sink we learn one way *not* to walk on water, and that is a key ingredient to our success. The truth is, our real failure is not in sinking or falling down, but in refusing to get back up and try again. I guess that was the difference between Judas and Peter. They both did horrible things. Judas betrayed the Lord and Peter denied Him. But the difference was that one gave up and hung himself, while the other received forgiveness and started over.

Proverbs 24:16 says a godly man may trip seven times, but each time he will rise again. That's why people relate to Peter. He fell a lot, but he kept getting up. And that's why people love David too. He made a lot of mistakes, but he kept on loving God. The difference between the giants of faith and the dwarves of faith is not that one falls and the other doesn't, the difference is one has learned the art of getting back up while the other stays down.

The key is not not falling down, but learning how to get up again.

Getting up isn't easy. It's really, really hard. It separates the men from the boys. If you've seen *Rocky 2* you know what I'm talking about. At the end of the match between Rocky and Apollo, Rocky lands a punch that knocks Apollo down. But Rocky was so beat up and tired that he fell down too. They both lie on the floor at the same time. But then Apollo tries to get up. He climbs up the ropes . . . but collapses at the last second. Rocky also climbs up the ropes, only he doesn't give up. He stood wearily to his feet at the last possible second, and won the match. Rocky and Apollo both fell equally hard, but Rocky was declared the champion not because he didn't fall, but because he could get back up.

If you want to be great, you're going to fall hard. You can count on that. Rocky would have never fallen if he didn't attempt fighting a world champion. But he wouldn't have been remembered either. If you don't attempt great things you may not have "great" failures, but you'll never accomplish anything great either.

Too often we don't attempt to walk on water because we're afraid of sinking. We don't try to succeed because we're afraid of failure. Remember, Peter was the only one to sink in the story. The other disciples didn't sink. But they didn't walk on water either.

I read this really cool statistic a while back about Reggie Jackson. Remember him, the New York Yankees baseball player from the 70s? He's a legend. They used to call him Mr. October because he was so clutch in the play-offs. He was a 4 time American League homerun champion, a 5 time World Series champion, a 14 time All Star selection, an MVP winner and a hall of famer. But do you know that Reggie Jackson is also the leading strikeout hitter *of all time?*

But do you consider him a failure?

You know, I could boast that I've struck out less times than Reggie Jackson. But I've never hit one out of the park. And that just shows me the bigger the giant is, the harder he will fall. So listen to me. Don't be afraid to swing for the fences, because all those strikeouts are worth that one game-winning homerun. All those hard knocks are worth the gold medal around your neck. All those failed attempts at the light bulb are worth changing the world. And all those times you sink are worth the one time you walk on water.

Failure is required for success, so step out, because life is too short to stay inside the boat of complacency.

Chapter 14

Superheroes

We've all had our superheroes growing up. One of my favorites was Raphael the Ninja Turtle. As a little kid I recall having a giant Raphael stuffed turtle. He was bigger than me. I loved to carry him around with me places until my arms got tired. Raphael was the man (or should I say, "the turtle") because he could defeat innumerable foes with his sai (those spork-looking weapons). He was so unstoppable and so cool when he would beat back all of Shredder's goons.

Shortly after that, when the Power Rangers were invented, I became a huge fan of the Red Power Ranger. His moves were sensational. No matter how many bad guys came at him, you could be sure the Red Power Ranger would come out on top. And whenever lives were at stake, just call on Jason (that was his name), and he could put on his outfit and save the day.

Every little boy has his favorite superhero. And no matter how bad things get, we know our favorite superhero won't die. Even if it seems like he dies, we know someone will bust out a defibrillator and pump him back to life. We know he's got to show up for the next episode . . . because how could the show go on if he's dead? So we keep watching. We keep watching him risk his life for the sake of others, yet somehow never disappoint us by dying. This inspires us.

But it's not just little boys who have their favorite heroes. Little girls do too, just in a different way. Each little girl has her own special prince. A prince who is charming, yet brave. Powerful, yet selfless with his power. Thick of skin, but tender of heart. And this heroic prince is always quite the romantic! He can quote a poem and speak French in one scene, but have blood dripping down his face after slaying a hundred men in the next. And no matter what, he's always, always driven by love for a woman. So he will fight a dragon for his damsel in distress, and after he slays the foul beast, he will share a happily ever after with her. Every time.

So I'm pretty sure that God is the One who gave kids their love for superheroes. My philosophy is that He's the One behind it all. As little guys, we can't explain *why* we have such desires . . . we just know we do. And the truth is, our "childish" passions don't go away once we get older. We still believe in super-heroes as grown-ups; we believe there's someone out there who has the power to rescue us from the human struggle . . .

Someone like that boss who has the "power" to hire you on to your dream job. That husband who could be your Prince Charming. That popular kid at school who has the superpower of "coolness," and maybe he could ask you to be his friend and you would be rescued at last!

It's not bad to want a superhero to rescue us. Even as adults, it's a good desire to have. But the problem is we look to the wrong people to be our super-heroes. The people we look to are not only *not* superheroes, they're actually the victims. They're just like us. Flawed and needy. And as much as you may think, "If only this girl would go out with me, I'd be rescued from my misery!" she can't save you.

There has only been one Superhero who has ever walked the planet. Unlike Raphael the Ninja Turtle, He walked the face of the earth in reality and not just in fiction. God entrusted to this Man superhuman powers. He could walk on water, pass through locked doors, float up to the sky, and disappear. The Superhero I'm speaking of is more graceful than Prince Charming. More mighty than Superman. More courageous than Batman . . .

His name is Jesus Christ.

And in John 16:33, Jesus Christ made the most incredible superhero statement of all time . . .

"In the world you will have tribulation, but be of good cheer, *I have overcome the world.*"

I mean, who says that? I have overcome the *world?* Anyone who makes that claim is either a megalomaniac or the Son of God. All heroes could say they've overcome some stuff. The Turtles could say they overcame Shredder. The Power Rangers could say they overcame the evil witch Rita Repulsa. Sonic the Hedgehog could say he overcame Dr. Robotnik. But only the greatest Superhero of all time could dare to say, "I have overcome the world."

But what does that mean? Jesus has overcome the world? William Barclay explained this superhero statement well when he said, "The world could do it's worst to Jesus and still not defeat Him." Think about it. The world threw its worst temptations at Jesus and He never sinned. The world threw its worst torture chamber at Jesus (a slow and painful death) but *he charged straight for the cross!* The world threw death at Jesus, but He beat that too. There's nothing, nothing in *all the world*, that Jesus couldn't beat.

And listen. The good news gets even better. Jesus said He conquered the world, so Paul jumps on this and says in Romans 8:37 that "*we* are more than conquerors through *Him* who loved us."

"Wait a second," you say. "*I* am more than a conqueror? Me? Really? How can that be?" Because Jesus conquered the world and *you are in Him*, you are more than a conqueror by default!

It's kind of like this. Have you ever been on a team where there was a star player who seemed to score all the points? He was just so good that he literally carried your team? Well, Jesus is that star Player. He scores a hundred points a game. And because you and I have said, "Umm . . . I'll be on His team!" We get the gold medals around our necks because He wins all our games for us! Therefore *we* are more than conquerors! Isn't that awesome?

Never forget that Jesus overcame the world without our help. He doesn't *need* us to be on His team. But He's so nice that He invites us to play with Him even though we're terrible. We're always turning the ball over and scoring for the wrong team. We miss our shots. But Jesus never does. Not even once.

Doesn't Jesus just put all the other superheroes to shame? I mean, He's a champion who picks losers to be on His team. He's a ferocious warrior and yet loves our souls like the most sensitive romantic. He's got the thickest skin and the softest heart. And He will never die. He always shows up for the next episode. He risked His life, *gave* His life, and yet He lives on. And they didn't even need a defibrillator to bring Him back!

My point is that I think God put in us the love for superheroes to point us to Jesus. To show us that He is the true Superhero we've been longing for since childhood. Every quality Raphael, Superman, or Prince Charming has is found in Him and exceeded by Him. Sonic the Hedgehog can't save us from the human struggle . . . and neither can your future husband. Only Jesus can. He is that Prince who defeats the Great Dragon to save us, the damsels in distress. And as hard as it is to believe that Someone *so* perfect could be real, Jesus isn't fiction.

And yet my problem is this. It makes sense that Jesus can have super-powers because He's the Son of God, for crying out loud. What gets me is that it seems like the rest of the Bible characters had superpowers too! I mean, a fisherman walks on the sea he fishes on? A guy gets bit by a deadly snake and shakes it off? Three friends hang out in a deadly furnace without being burnt? It kind of seems like they were all superheroes living in a fantasy world.

But they weren't. *They were humans just like us.* So how did they do such fantastical things? What was their secret?

Good question. The secret of these Bible characters was not that they had any superpowers of their own . . . they just happened to have a Superhero God *whose power they tapped into!* All they did was pass the ball to their Star Player and let Him score all the points for them.

This really encourages me because sometimes I look at Elijah and Moses and say, "I could never be like them. They were superhuman." But the truth is they were just like me. The key to the great Bible characters was not their abilities, *but their faith in their Superhero's abilities.* This gives me hope because I don't have to rely on my silly little abilities to do great things. All I have to do is respond in faith to God's abilities. As Corrie ten Boom said, "It is not my ability, but my response to God's ability that counts." It's true I'm a really big failure, but I just so happen to have a really big God.

Listen. The superpowers of the Bible characters are available to Ben Courson, and to you, the one reading this book. Isn't that crazy? Think of the power that Peter had. Stephen had. Paul had. These men knew that, *through Jesus,* they were super-conquerors, hence Paul's statement, "I can do all things *through Christ* who strengthens me." This power is yours to tap into simply by having faith in your Superhero.

And yet we live in a culture that tells us to believe in ourselves. Let me just tell you that "believing in yourself" doesn't work. I've tried it before. Trust me, believing in Jesus works a lot better. And if you will believe in Him enough to pass the ball of your life into His hands, He will swish it every time. Your faith in Him can even give you the superpower of tossing mountains into the sea!

Jedi Master Qui-Gon Jinn once told young Anakin Skywalker, "Your focus determines your reality." I love that quote. It's true, what you focus on determines what your reality will be. Focus on yourself, and you'll be depressed. Focus on the stormy circumstances around you, and like Peter, you will "sink" into depression. Focus on Jesus, and walking on waves will be like walking on the sidewalk.

Chapter 15

David and the Grasshopper

So my favorite basketball team, the Los Angeles Lakers, beat the Celtics a few weeks back in game 7 of the NBA finals. Kobe didn't have his best shooting night, but he grabbed 15 boards to make up for it, and was awarded with the MVP. It was a very entertaining game because neither team was at their best, so they resorted to playing sloppy and passionate basketball. Those are the funnest games to watch. When it all comes down to who wants it more.

As me and my dad sat on the couch and took it all in, I was amazed at how emotional the Lakers got once the buzzer went off. Here were these giant warriors in yellow jerseys, crying and giving each other big sweaty bear hugs as confetti fell from above. Kobe was standing on a table and pumping his fist at the crowd. Lamar Odom was hugging three players simultaneously. Ron Artest was so happy he could hardly focus during his interview (the reporter asked him what kind of satisfaction he took in being able to support Kobe, and he answered the question by saying, "First of all, I want to thank everyone in my hood"). Obviously these guys were completely overwhelmed.

This always seems to happen when championships are won. Grown men get really emotional, hug each other, and put on their happy hats. They float on cloud nine and celebrate as if they had just got done conquering the world itself. But have you ever noticed how players never celebrate with this kind of passion after they win a regular season game? When the Lakers beat the worst team in the league they'll be happy for sure, but they won't be bear hugging and weeping and standing on tables.

Why is this? Because if the Lakers beat a team that doesn't provide much of a challenge, there's no trophy involved and therefore the victory isn't as sweet. Little opposition brings little reward. But when they beat the NBA's toughest team, like the Celtics, they'll never forget it, because *the harder the challenge is, the more rewarding the victory will be.*

It's kind of funny when you stop to think about how every team's goal is to make it to the championship, the most challenging game of all. They work as hard as they can to put themselves in the hardest place possible! They *want* the most brutal test. They want it because they know if they can pass it, they will be rewarded with the biggest trophy.

This principle is no different in life. The harder our challenges are, the sweeter our victories will be. I think that's why the Bible uses sports analogies like boxing, wrestling, and running (basketball wasn't around back then). In sports, athletes *crave* the most difficult tests to get the best prizes. And as Christians, we will be the happiest when we strive for the toughest challenges and overcome. We won't be happy if we seek a trouble-free life. If our aim is to relax, play Play Station 3, and live the easy life, the reward will be small because there is little opposition.

This is exactly why no one knows the story of David and the Grasshopper. I bet you David killed a grasshopper (or at least a bug) at some point in his life. But if he did, no one remembers it. Why? Because there's no challenge in killing a bug. But *everyone* knows the story of David and Goliath. Why do they know that one? Because David faced the hardest opponent in all the world and beat him. That's why he's a champion.

Remember how last chapter I talked about how we are champions because Jesus overcame the world for us? Well, there was something I left out. Something very important. Right before Jesus made the superhero statement, "I have overcome the world," He said, "in the world you will have tribulation." That was the part I left out. We all like the "overcoming" part. But not very many people are big fans of the "tribulation" part. Everyone wants to be a champion . . . but not everyone is willing to face the tribulation it takes to get there.

To be honest, I'm glad Jesus said what He did. I'm glad He promised us tribulation. Because if there were no real challenge or hardship, then the reward would be pretty puny. Think about it. Alexander the Great didn't become Alexander the Great by fighting a few puny opponents. No. He had to go up against the powerhouses of the world to become the conqueror he's remembered as today. The same is true for us. We can't be super-conquerors unless we're fighting super big battles.

That's why I think it's silly when I complain about how brutal my problems are. The Lord would say, "Ben, didn't you ask for huge victories? You can't get a huge trophy unless you face huge opposition." 28.2 million people don't tune in to watch the Lakers play the last-place team, but they sure do when they play the Celtics! And the world won't tune into Jesus if His followers are killing grasshoppers, but they sure will if they see us killing giants!

The harder the challenge is, the more rewarding the victory will be.

One of the greatest rewards I ever got in life came from one of my greatest challenges. When I was in high school, I had dated a girl on and off (I'm pretty sure dating doesn't work now that I look back on it, but that's just my opinion) and I liked her but it seemed like there was something missing. When I moved back to Oregon, we were clicking less and less. So we broke up. We both moved on shortly after and lived our separate lives, and things seemed to be going fine.

But nearly a year later, my heart completely changed. One day in December my feelings toward her started flooding in. I thought I was falling in love, and I was convinced she was the girl I was supposed to marry. So I drove twelve hours to take her to dinner.

We sat down at a table in a Mexican restaurant, and I told her I was in love with her.

But she didn't feel the same way. At all. In fact, she ended up getting together with my best friend. And my heart wasn't just broken, it was shattered. For a whole year I was in survival mode. My goal wasn't to thrive in life, I just wanted to survive each day. I remember that I couldn't wait until the night would come so I could sleep away the pain. But then I started getting nightmares, and sleeping wasn't all that fun anymore. I couldn't escape. I felt like I was drowning in an ocean of tears, and the current of pain just kept pulling me further out to sea.

I was falling deeper and deeper into depression. No matter how badly I wanted to get over it, I couldn't. I felt silly being so broken over a girl, and that made the suffering feel even worse. It wasn't like I was suffering because I preached about Jesus and got rocks thrown at me. Nor was I suffering over the death of a loved one. It was over a girl who didn't like me. And I felt like a silly pile of worthless trash. I know that's kind of intense. But that's how I felt.

But then the Lord came in. As I hung on the end of my rope, not knowing if I could hang on any longer, Jesus picked me up and rescued me. The means of deliverance He used was very different than what I would have expected. His deliverance took on the form of a godly, beautiful blonde-haired girl. It was on a Wednesday night, and my dad had just concluded the Bible study. I saw Necia hanging out in the sanctuary all pretty and quiet-like, and I was star-struck. Now we were already friends and had known each other for a few years, but when I saw her that night, something clicked inside of me. Right then I knew I had to do something about it. I thought to myself, "I've got to take her to Taco Bell!"

So that's what I did. We went to Taco Bell. And several months later, she became my wife.

Me and Necia have been married for almost two years now, and God hasn't just met my expectations, He's surpassed them. All the while I was heart-broken over my old girlfriend, God was secretly preparing for me the wife of my dreams. It's funny because when me and Necia were kids, my mom and her mom would pray together that we would grow up to marry just the right person. Little did they know we would marry each other! Isn't God just amazing?

Please hear me on this. The very door that was closed to my old girlfriend was an open door to Necia all along, because *the doors that God closes are really just open doors in disguise.* When the door was slammed in my face, I was in despair. But I failed to realize that the harder a door slams in my face, the more beautiful it will be when it opens! I thought if I couldn't have my girlfriend back I was going to die. But little did I know God was waiting to reveal a girl that was infinitely more perfect for me, a girl He created specifically just for Ben. And when the door opened to Necia, suddenly it all made sense.

See, God is in the business of turning tragedies into triumphs. A lot of times people go through hard times and say, "there must be a reason for this tragedy." No. There's not just a reason for your tragedy, your tragedy *is* the reason itself, because your tragedy is a triumph in disguise! The very door that is slammed in your face is actually an open door to something far greater. That's why you can rejoice whenever a door closes to something you want, because that means God has something even better He wants to open up for you! As Helen

Keller said, "When one door of happiness closes, another opens; but often we look so long at the closed door that we do not see the one which has been opened up for us."

A perfect example of this is Paul the Apostle. He wanted so badly to preach to the Jews, but the Jews kept on rejecting his message. He would've done anything to see them saved. He even said he was willing to be cut off from Christ if only that could help bring them to Jesus. But they slammed the door in his face. Finally he told them, "Since you have rejected it (the Gospel) and judged yourselves unworthy of eternal life - well, we will offer it to Gentiles."

The closed door to the Jews, who Paul wanted to reach so badly, became the open door to the rest of the world! God had something even bigger in store for Paul than Paul had in mind for his own ministry. Had Paul had success among the Jews, he would have focused more on them and less on the rest of planet earth, and the world would've missed out on the Gospel!

But Paul isn't the only Bible character who had a door slammed in his face before he reached his destiny. The truth is, most Bible characters went through hell before they got blessed: Ruth lost the husband of her youth before she met Boaz, the heroic man who would redeem her. Job lost his health, all his money, and his kids before he reached the peak of his prosperity. Joseph had to live in a dungeon before he became Prime Minister of Egypt. David spent most of his youth running for his life as a refugee before he was crowned king. Jesus had to die on a cross before He rose again in a glorified body.

The godliest men and women faced the worst kinds of tragedies, but their tragedies were turned into triumphs. It's not just that triumph came out of their tragedy. No, the tragedies themselves were actually *transformed* into triumphs. *The very thing* that Satan meant for evil in each of their lives was the very thing

God meant for good.

Think of the cross itself. Today the cross is the greatest symbol of triumph known to mankind, but it wasn't always that way. For a few days it was the worst symbol of tragedy the world had ever known. When Jesus was lying in the grave, if you talked about "the cross" around His followers, they would've burst into tears. I bet it was something you just wouldn't bring up. The cross brought nothing but pain to Jesus' disciples. Horrific pain. It represented the bloody murder of their Savior.

But three days after Jesus hung on that cross, the symbol of greatest sadness became the symbol of greatest joy. The tragedy was a triumph in disguise all along. Now people wear crosses around their necks. They build crosses in the middle of cities. They tattoo crosses on their bodies. It seems people just can't get enough of the cross now!

Listen to me, the doors that break your heart now will prove to be the open doors to what your heart is truly craving. Your greatest sorrows in life are simply the pathways to your sweetest victories. And the worst pain you feel is the very thing that grows you into the person you need to be for your destiny.

I remember when I was a kid I used to get crazy growing pains. Sports Cream was my best friend back in the day because it was the only thing that soothed my aching legs. At the time, I hated growing pains. I wished so bad I didn't have them. But as Chuck Smith would say, "Hindsight is always better than foresight," and as I look back, I'm really glad I had growing pains. If my bones and joints never grew and stretched, I may have had little pain, but I would have stayed two feet tall. Now that I'm an adult I see that I needed the stretching, I needed the pain, or else I never would have grown. So too, the painful experiences in your life are really just hidden blessings sent to grow you.

But you know what was funny about my growing pains? I never woke up in the morning, looked in the mirror, and thought, "Hey, I'm taller than I was yesterday. It must have been those growing pains I had last night!" It was never like that. I never once saw my own growth. But it didn't matter, because I was growing whether I saw it or not.

You may be in pain right now wondering what it's all for. But I'm telling you, whether or not you see your own growth, your suffering is making you a giant of faith. Nothing grows you faster than pain. Just look around at creation and you'll know I'm telling the truth . . .

How do flowers grow? They grow by getting rained on a lot. How does a refiner purify gold? By burning it with fire. When do stars shine the brightest? When the night is the darkest. How are diamonds made? By undergoing intense pressure. How does a caterpillar force enough ichor into its wings so it can fly? By painfully struggling all by itself out of the cocoon.

The same is true for you. You won't fly like a butterfly until you struggle all by yourself. You won't sparkle like a diamond until people put pressure on you. You won't shine as bright as the stars until you've been through the dark night of fear. You won't be pure like gold until you get burned by fiery trials. You won't have the beauty of a flower until you get rained on by the cloud that hovers over you wherever you go.

You need the pain. It's the only way you'll grow. I know you may hate the storm you're in. I know you may be scared to death. But the waves that threaten to kill you will actually become the very platforms that let you walk on water. So don't just tread water, tread *upon* the water! Life was never about surviving, it's about thriving. So embrace your challenge. Embrace your pain. Because the *harder the challenge is, the more rewarding the victory will be.*

So send the giants, Lord, because I don't want to go down as a grass-hopper killer. I want to be a giant killer. It's time to stop measuring the size of my giant and start measuring the size of my God.

Chapter 16

Whom the Lord Loveth He Kicketh

I used to look at certain people and think that nothing could faze them. That no matter what giants they faced, they'd win guaranteed. I used to think that some people were naturals at being supernatural and were unaffected by fear and pain.

But this isn't the truth.

No one has disinhyperated lungs . . .

Let me explain. The summer going into my freshman year of high school, my family and I moved to Orange County. I was new and didn't know anyone, but I met a guy named Travis on the football field who befriended me and was really cool to me. We ended up becoming good friends all throughout high school, and some of the funniest life memories I have were spent with him.

One of my favorites was when I had him over for one of the first times. I had just moved into the new house, and I was so stoked because we had a pool and hot tub in our backyard. Now, I had learned a little Oregonian trick before I moved. One of my buddies had taught me how to breathe under water in hot tubs. If you've never done this, you may not believe me, but it's true. In certain hot tubs there are air holes on the floor or on the seats, and if you turn on the jets oxygen will come splurting out. You can put your mouth over the hole and suck in the air and actually breathe underwater. It's pretty sweet. One time I was under there for probably forty minutes, and I almost fell asleep because it was so relaxing. You can literally spend hours without coming up to the surface. Anyone can do this, although I'm not sure you should try this at home because I don't know how healthy it is.

Well the hot tub at our new house happened to have air holes. So I decided to play a little trick on Travis. I told him I had this crazy condition called disinhyperated lungs (which isn't a real word, I just made it up) and I asked him if he'd heard of it. "Oh yeah man," he said, "for sure." I told him this is why I could breathe under water and run for hours without getting tired. So I decided to put my disinhyperated lungs on display. I went underwater and started breathing the air holes on the floor while the jets covered my body so he couldn't see what I was doing. I popped up maybe twenty minutes later, and I wasn't even breathing heavy. Obviously Travis was bewildered. He thought I really did have a crazy disease that let me to do the impossible like breathing under water.

After I got a good kick out of it I told him that I didn't really have disinhyperated lungs and that I made the word up. I explained to him how the trick worked, and he discovered that I wasn't any different from anyone else.

No one has disinhyperated lungs. I know it seems like there are special humans who can do the impossible; it seems like no matter what they go through, nothing can drown them. But it isn't true. *Everybody* is needy and gulping for air. Searching for meaning. Longing for hope. Everybody feels the pain and knows what it's like to be scared to death.

You know who I would've thought had disinhyperated lungs? Paul the Apostle. I mean the guy could do crazy things. He'd share the Gospel and people would throw rocks at him, snakes would bite him, whips would lash his back, jailers threw him behind bars . . . but he kept on preaching. He was ridiculous. Nothing could stop him. And if you only read the book of Acts you'd think pain and fear didn't even affect him. But it's a good thing he wrote letters, so we can see what was *really* going on with Paul the Apostle.

In a letter he wrote to the Corinthians, he penned one of my all-time favorite passages (these verses have changed my life): "To keep me from getting puffed up, I was given a thorn in my flesh, a messenger from Satan to torment me and keep me from getting proud. Three different times I begged the Lord to take it away. Each time He said, 'My gracious favor is all you need. My power works best in your weakness.' So now I am glad to boast about my weaknesses, so that the power of Christ may work through me. Since I know it is all for Christ's good, I am quite content with my weaknesses and with insults, hardships, persecutions, and calamities. For when I am weak, then I am strong." In these epic verses, Paul lets us in on his secret. He shows us how he could go through such beatings without drowning in them. He says, "My strength isn't magic. I don't have disinhyperated lungs or anything. I've just found that Jesus Christ is an outside source of oxygen that fills my lungs when all I want to do is lie down and die."

Paul felt weak just like you and me. *But he learned that the weaker he was, the more he had to lean on Jesus, and the more he leaned on Jesus, the stronger he became!* That made him like those blow-up boxing clowns: the harder you hit him, the faster he popped up! You just couldn't keep the guy down.

He reminds me a lot of baby giraffes. A few months ago I came across an online page that had an amazing fact about these little fellas. Craig B. Larson pulls from the book *A View From The Zoo* (written by Gary Richmond) to vividly describe what happens when these funny animals are introduced to the world:

"A baby giraffe falls 10 feet from its mother's womb and usually lands on its back. Within seconds it rolls over and tucks its legs under its body. From this position it considers the world for the first time and shakes off the last vestiges of the birthing fluid from its eyes and ears. Then the mother giraffe rudely introduces its offspring to the reality of life…The mother giraffe lowers her head long enough to take a quick look. Then she positions herself directly over her calf. She waits for about a minute, and then she does the most unreasonable thing. She swings her long, pendulous leg outward and kicks her baby, so that it is sent sprawling head over heels."

(Could you imagine if your mom did that to *you* right after you were born? *Boom!* Drop kicked out of the hospital room).

"When it doesn't get up, the violent process is repeated over and over again. The struggle to rise is momentous. As the baby calf grows tired, the mother kicks it again to stimulate its efforts. Finally, the calf stands for the first time on it's wobbly legs.

"Then the mother giraffe does the most remarkable thing. She kicks it off its feet again. Why? She wants it to remember how it got up. In the wild, baby giraffes must be able to get up as quickly as possible to stay with the herd, where there is safety. Lions, hyenas, leopards, and wild hunting dogs all enjoy young giraffes, and they get it too, if the mother didn't teach her calf to get up quickly and get with it."

Larson then went on to talk about a man named Irving Stone who understood, like baby giraffes, the lesson of getting back up. Stone spent his life studying great men, and he even wrote some novelized biographies about them (such as Michelangelo and Vincent van Gogh). He was once asked if he'd found a thread that runs through the lives of the greats, and his answer was beautiful: "I write about people who sometime in their life have a vision or dream of something that should be accomplished and they go to work. They are beaten over the head, knocked down, vilified, and for years they get nowhere. But every time they're knocked down they stand up. You cannot destroy these people. And at the end of their lives they've accomplished some modest part of what they set out to do."

Even the greats fall down. No, let me re-phrase that. Especially the greats fall down. They get hit hard. But what makes them legends is that they've mastered the art of getting back up.

I find it interesting that lions will eat the baby giraffes who don't learn to get back up after they're kicked. I point this out because the Bible describes Satan as a roaring lion who is looking for people to devour. And who are the ones he snacks on for lunch? The ones who stay down, the ones who lie there like dead meat because they refuse to learn the lesson of perseverance.

So, after I learned all this about giraffes, I gained a new respect for their mamas. At first you think the mamas are jerks, but then you find out the reason they kick their babies is because they love them.

And the truth is a lot of people think God is a jerk. They get knocked around like a soccer ball and question His compassion. They think God is violent and unfair. But you know what God would say in response?

"Whom I loveth I kicketh."

Isn't it so cool how God can use animals to teach us some of His most profound lessons? Giraffes make sense of Hebrews 12:6, which says, "For whom the Lord loveth He chasteneth, and scourgeth every son whom He receiveth." How do you know if you're one of God's kids? If He kicks you around. If He's tough on you, it's because He's training you to persevere and survive in a savage world.

You know, I bet you baby giraffes aren't too happy with their mamas when they're getting clobbered on day one. But down the road it'll make sense to them, so much so that when they grow older they will do the very same thing to their younglings.

The reality is, it would be cruel for the mother *not* to kick her child. Little giraffes aren't like bears or rattlesnakes, they're not great warriors, so they need to find an alternative way to survive. That's why the mother will kick her baby, so it can learn to get up quick enough to stay close to the herd, where it finds strength in numbers. So too, I'm like the giraffe. I may never be a great warrior, but it doesn't matter. My strength is not in my abilities. My strength is in my weakness, in my need to stay close to Jesus. And as long as I'm with Him, I have strength of numbers.

Now, when the roaring lion sees me, he's going to run for his life.

Chapter 17

Know God, No Fear. No God, Know Fear.

Winston Churchill once said, "A pessimist sees the difficulty in every opportunity; an optimist sees the opportunity in every difficulty." All over the pages of the Bible we are encouraged to be optimists. To hope in God, no matter how hard things get. The problem is, having a hopeful, optimistic perspective flies in the face of the culture we're living in. The world around us is constantly speaking negativity into our lives. Just watch the news and you'll know I'm speaking the truth. The world is cynical. Disillusioned. Depressed. That's why in the last six chapters I've been fighting for hope, fighting for us to dream big for God and to never, ever give up. No matter what.

But now I must warn you. If you put into practice the extreme hope of the Bible we've been talking about, I guarantee you you're going to get hit for it . . . hard. Dreamers never have it easy. If you have the courage to be a hopeful person, lots of people will simply dismiss you as naive and ignorant. They'll tell you your faith is a crutch. A cop out. A denial of reality.

But I'm here to tell you this . . .

Who cares what they think?

Being scared of what others think about us is silly. Yet for some reason we all struggle with it. I've struggled with it all my life. Big time. But the older I get the more I realize how stupid it is to define who I am based on what anyone else says. When I have the Lord's favor, the opinions of mere people don't matter a bit.

To illustrate my point, I remember a few summers back I was really into sour strips. They were by far my favorite candy. You can buy them at Candy Tyme in the mall, and they make your taste buds party like there's no tomorrow. I used to eat them all the time. I've stopped now because I'm *trying* to be more nutritious, seeing I've been a junk food addict most my life. But I'll never forget the heavenly taste of those strawberry sour strips. My mouth is watering even as I write.

Well one summer evening I was hanging out with my sister Mary, and all the sudden I got this fierce craving for sour strips. This wasn't abnormal, however, because I used to get urges for them on a regular basis (Mary gets sudden urges too, only not for sour strips; her cravings are for Diet Coke. She needs her Diet Coke). This particular evening I was dying to have some sour strips, but it was getting late, and I feared that maybe Candy Tyme would be closed. So Mary called the mall to ask what time it was open till, and thank goodness we still had a few minutes to blitz over there!

We left my apartment and drove to the mall, but we accidentally parked quite a distance from Candy Tyme. So me and Mary burst through the doors and literally started sprinting through the food court and past the stores towards our destination. People must've been wondering why in the world we were racing through the building like that, but it didn't matter because I had to get my strips. We finally arrived at the candy store huffing and puffing and sweaty. *Yes! Just in time!*

I spotted the strips, purchased them, then scarfed them down. It was heavenly. I was so caught up in the deliciousness of my snack that I couldn't care less what the people in the mall thought about me. I'm sure they thought I was ridiculous. Here I was, an adult running through the mall like a mad man to get *candy*. I bet as I zoomed by the shoppers they thought I was late for something very grown-up and important (after all, I *was* running as if I was tardy to a meeting with the president). But when they saw me race into the candy store and realized *that's* where I was off to, they probably thought I was pretty childish.

But their opinion of me didn't matter. Why? Because I wanted my treat so bad that I didn't care how stupid I looked in trying to get it. And once I put the candy in my mouth, I was too enraptured in my pleasure to even notice them.

The same is true spiritually. When we want Jesus so badly that we actually *crave* Him, we will be so busy scarfing on Him that we won't even have an appetite for the approval of people. We may look silly chasing after Him, but we won't care, because He's just *so* satisfying.

I love how the Bible likens spirituality to scrumptious food. The psalmist told us to *taste* and see the goodness of the Lord. His goodness tastes like strawberry sour strips. The Bible also says His Word is *sweeter than honey*. Or I might say in my language that His Word is even more toothsome than Taco Bell (my favorite restaurant). Jeremiah said, "Your words were found, and I *ate* them." In other words, the Scriptures are so good you can devour them like you'd devour your favorite novel. Jesus told us to *eat* His body. Just as we need food to sustain our bodies, when we eat Jesus He sustains our souls. But my favorite is Matthew 5:6, where Jesus told us to *hunger* for righteousness. We should *crave* it. The same way I craved my Candy Tyme treat. And Jesus promised us that if we are hungry for righteousness, we'll be *filled*. Our souls will be stuffed, just like my belly was after I gobbled down my candy.

The reality is everyone is craving approval from someone. Some people crave the approval and applause of humans and find out it's like cotton candy, not filling at all. Others crave the applause of God, which fills them like ProTex power bars. When I feast on His favor, my heart is so stuffed it *can't* crave people's favor. I just won't have an appetite for anything else because I'm so glutted on Him.

My friend Xav knows this to be true. He's one of the most interesting people I know. He could've gone pro as a Razor Scooterist in high school, but turned it down because he wanted to graduate instead. He then went to Bible college in Hawaii, which was fully paid for by a guy who was an *atheist.* Next, he started teaching at the Bible college even though he was still college age. He's got the hugest hair you've ever seen, wears the craziest clothes (he used to wear Ferret fur), has a tiny dog named Francois, is a slack-liner . . . and also happens to be one of the greatest young Bible teachers I've ever heard. Right now he's teaching the Bible to the youth at my home church, but is planning to travel around Europe in a few months with his brother to sleep under the Eiffel Tower, eat food at random people's houses, and share the Gospel with everyone he sees. He told me, "Everyone talks about doing great things for God, but don't actually *do* anything. So I decided to go out and attempt something big for Him." He said this with no fear in his eyes.

Xav does crazy things all the time because he doesn't care what anyone thinks about him. I don't know if it's just because he's super brave, or because the fear of man simply doesn't register with him. Either way, he's not afraid of what people think of him . . . at all.

One day he told me a really cool quote he'd heard: "Know God, no fear. No God, know fear." Because Xav lives in the fear of God, he cannot live in the fear of man. Every human must choose whom he will fear. Either God or man. You cannot fear both simultaneously. As Oswald Chambers put it, "The remarkable thing about fearing God is that when you fear God you fear nothing else, whereas if you do not fear God you fear everything else."

The secret to not fearing people is to get close to God, because when you do, He will fill your craving for affirmation with His love, and your appetite for man's approval will suddenly vanish. Like a magic trick. And it works every time.

It's kind of like this. Imagine you're a high schooler who lives in LA and dreams of one day becoming an actor. You decide to try out for the school play for starters, and you win the lead role! You can hardly contain your happiness, so you practice and rehearse and give your all to learning how to act. So when the big day finally rolls around, you're ready. You have a blast, and in your heart you know this is what you're supposed to do with your life.

But after the play is over, as you hang out in the auditorium and talk with the other drama kids, one of the school's popular jocks sees you. You hear him and his friends making fun of you and laughing at your performance when they think you're not listening. And with every word they say your heart is breaking.

You drive home depressed, broken over what the popular kids said. You go straight to your room and lie on your bed, brooding over your hurt. Suddenly your phone vibrates. A local number pops up on your screen that you don't recognize. You pick up . . . and you cannot believe who is on the other end.

It's your favorite movie star.

"I was shooting a scene downtown today," he says, "and I decided to go for a walk through the city once I was finished. I just so happened to walk past your school, and I saw a sign that said there was a play going on inside. I thought I'd stop by and sit in the back for a few minutes. I watched your performance, and I must say . . . you were brilliant. I loved your work so much that I snuck over to your drama teacher afterwards to ask for your phone number to tell you how impressed I was and hook you up with some auditions, that is, if you're interested."

You can't believe your ears. All of a sudden you couldn't care less what that mean popular kid said about you. Why? Because you just got applause from a movie star! And the movie star's opinion completely overshadows the opinion of the school bully.

When you hear the God who created Mars and gophers and waterfalls say to you, "I think you're amazing, and I have plans to prosper you," suddenly everyone else's opinions of you won't matter a whit. In fact, you'll find it rather humorous that you ever feared little humans when you realize the King of kings was hooking you up with His favor all along.

Paul the Apostle understood this. He didn't even *want* people to sing his praises. Because he feared the Lord so much he was completely immune to the fear of man. I'll show you what I mean. In Acts 14, when Paul was preaching in the city of Lystra, he noticed a crippled man in the crowd. He saw that this man had the faith to be healed, so he told him to stand up. It didn't matter that the guy had been paralyzed from birth, he just got up and started walking around! The people of Lystra saw this, and immediately they worshipped Paul, thinking he was one of their Greek gods come down in the flesh. They tried to offer sacrifices to him, but he tore his clothes and begged them to give the glory to God.

You're not going to believe what happened next. A few days after this miracle, some Jews from Antioch came to Lystra and persuaded the people to turn against Paul. So they did. They dragged him outside the city, threw rocks at him, and left him for dead. But Paul miraculously got up and dusted himself off. Then he went back into the city to keep on preaching! How sweet is that?

But it gets even better. Fourteen chapters later, in Acts 28, Paul was shipwrecked on an island. He was wet and cold, as was the rest of the crew, so he decided to go find some sticks to build a fire. But as he threw the sticks into the flames, he found that one of the sticks was actually a snake! It bit him and fastened its fangs into his skin. As it dangled from his hand, the islanders exclaimed, "Surely the gods are punishing this man, for he must be a murderer!" But Paul shook off the snake as though he were shaking off a fly. What a man! The islanders were wowed. They then hailed him as a god.

Did you catch the contrast? In Acts 14, the people of Lystra said, "Paul's a god!" only to later change their minds and say, "Paul's worthy of death!" The exact reverse of that happens in Acts 28: the islanders say, "Paul's worthy of death!" then they change their minds and say, "Paul's a god!" How funny are humans? One minute the people of Lystra think he's a god and then the next minute they try to kill him. One minute the islanders think Paul is worthy of death, then the next minute they try to worship him. They're all so fickle!

But we're no different from the islanders and the citizens of Lystra. One minute we exalt rock stars, actors, politicians, and athletes, but the next minute we change our minds, shove them off the platform, and move on to someone new. We lift people up as though they're divine, then forget about them completely once the Next Big Thing shows up. Then we repeat the process over and over again. It's pretty obvious that fickleness is simply *inbred* in the heart of every man.

People are flakey. Period. I am, and you are too. It's no wonder the Bible says, "Cursed is the man who trusts in man." If you want a curse to hang over your life, try and find security in what people think of you. They'll change their mind about you, trick you into thinking they like you when they actually don't, or act as though they think you're stupid when in reality they're just jealous. They will let you down and hurt you. Guaranteed. They're not trustworthy. There's no use in watering it down. Jesus Himself knew this to be true. In John 2:23-25 we're told that although people trusted in Him, He didn't trust *them*. Why? Because He knew what their hearts were really like: flakey and flawed. Good thing too, because one minute the Jews yelled "Hosanna" when He rode into town, and then only a few days later those same people yelled "crucify Him!" But He wasn't surprised. He was expecting it all along.

Man cannot be trusted. I'm not trying to be a humanity basher by saying that, believe me. So don't get me wrong. I think humans are some of the most beautiful of God's creation. Perhaps *the* most beautiful. In fact, sometimes I marvel at how unique and distinct human beings are from one another. Each one bears the image of God in a slightly different way than the other, revealing a side to the Lord that no one else can. And just as no two snowflakes are alike and all are beautiful, no two humans are alike and all are beautiful.

All I'm trying to say is that we may be beautiful and unique like snowflakes . . . but we're still flakes nonetheless.

Chapter 18

Empty Superstars

So whose applause are you after? God's or man's? If you think you can accomplish great things for the Lord while being scared to death of what humans think about you, all I have to say is - good luck. The fear of man has the power to paralyze even the strongest of men, that's why the giants of faith throughout history have deliberately refused to give into it.

I once heard a *hugely* influential pastor say, "If I worried about criticism I never would've done anything in life." If you listen to the taunts of fickle human beings, not only will you never do anything great in life, but you will actually waste your whole life bopping gators . . .

Here's what I mean. You know that game at the Family Fun Center where alligators come racing out of their little holes, and your goal is to bop as many of them with your hammer as you can? At first only one gator comes out, and it's pretty easy to smack him because he moves pretty slow. Then another one comes out, and you hit him too. But as the game progresses, the gators start popping out faster. Then a couple of them show their faces at the same time. Before you know it, four alligators are jumping out simultaneously, and your tired arm just can't keep up. You quickly discover that the longer you play the game, the more impossible it becomes.

This is exactly what the fear of man is like. You think, "if only this person liked me, then I'd be satisfied," so you bop approval out of them. The problem is, right after you get their approval, another person will pop up even quicker . . .

At first you just want the approval of that cool kid in your Science class. He starts warming up to you and you're stoked because you've put a point on the social scoreboard. But then you see that football player you admire, and you realize you need him to like you too. He gives you a compliment, and you're on to point number two. But you almost forgot about that girl at work who doesn't seem to like you, so you go out of your way to gain her favor. You get it, and you have three points. But there's a problem. You just found out that Kid # 1 (the cool kid in your Science class) said a word of gossip about you, so you go back to try and get him to warm up to you again. Then you realize the football player hasn't complimented you in a while, and you wonder if he's still impressed with you. But as you try to gain his praise, you notice your little brother hasn't been confiding in you lately. You fear that maybe he doesn't look up to you any more. And come to think of it, your best friend from church hasn't called in a while. Does he still like hanging out with you? And what about the girl you work with? What if her opinion of you changed over the past couple weeks?

Human praise will never be enough for you. Trust me, it's a game you just can't win. When you try to bop favor out of people you will find that, before you know it, there'll be so many faces popping up in your mind simultaneously that you won't be able to hammer down the approval of *any* of them. It's no wonder Proverbs 29:25 says the "fear of man is a trap."

But listen to what Proverbs 14:26 teaches: "In the fear of the Lord, there is strong confidence." What a contrast! While the fear of man traps you in a social game you just can't win, the fear of God bestows confidence on your soul. If you want to be an insecure, panicking person, be afraid of what people think. Try and bop approval out of everyone. But if you want an air of confidence about you, perform only for an audience of One. Fear God's opinion about you and no one else's, and I guarantee you a peace will radiate from you so strongly that more people will *want* to be around you than ever before. Let's be honest, it's a lot more satisfying to go after the approval of one God who loves us than it is to chase after one million people who don't know how to make up their minds.

That's why the most praised and admired people are often the most miserable. All the human praise they get is nothing more than cotton candy for their souls, so they're left *starving* for more. Ask Shia Labeouf. Shia Labeouf is the most famous young actor out there. He's only twenty-four years old, and his movies have already made billions of dollars. He's in blockbuster after blockbuster, he's Steven Spielberg's prodigy, and he's still just a kid. He's got it made. He's famous. Charming. Cool. And he's solidified himself as Hollywood's Next Big Thing.

But listen to what this wildly successful young movie star said in an interview with *Parade Magazine:* "Sometimes I feel like I'm living a meaningless life, and I get frightened." This is coming from the biggest box office star of our generation. "I don't handle fame well. Most actors on most days don't think they're worthy. I have no idea where this insecurity comes from, but it's a God-sized hole. If I knew, I'd fill it, and I'd be on my way." He also stated that the good actors are all in pain, and that his profession is one of "bottom-feeders and heartbroken people." He said he doesn't have a clue why he's an alcoholic, and when he asked himself what life is all about, he answered by saying, "I don't know."

Or look at Tom Brady. He's one of the best football quarterbacks of all time. He's won three Super Bowl rings, is married to a supermodel, is young, handsome, and charismatic, and he's also a millionaire. But in a *60 Minutes* interview, Brady said, "Why do I have three Super Bowl rings and still think there's something greater out there for me? I mean, maybe a lot of people would say, 'Hey man, this is what it is.' I reached my goal, my dream, my life. Me, I think, '…it's got to be more than this.' I mean this isn't, this can't be what it's all cracked up to be."

The interviewer then asked him, "What's the answer?"

"I wish I knew," he said. "I wish I knew. I love playing football and I love being quarterback for this team. But at the same time, I think there are a lot of other parts about me that I'm trying to find." Here's a legendary superstar quarterback who's got it all, but has found that gaining the world hasn't brought fulfillment to his soul.

Or even listen to the words of Chris Martin. Chris Martin is the lead singer of Coldplay, possibly the biggest rock band in the world. On one of his latest albums he sings, "time is so short and I'm sure there must be something more." And he's singing that even after he's sold tens of millions of records!

I think you get my point. Here are superstars who are empty. They've got all the praises of people. The masses scream their names. They've got everything a human being could ever want. But because they don't have Jesus, they are the first to admit that their souls are starving.

I'm sure there must be something more.

Chapter 19

The Answer to Every Problem

I'm reading through the Bible right now, and I happen to be in the book of Job. Yesterday I read a verse that seemed to be reading my mind. In chapter 6 verse 11, Job says, "I do not have the strength to endure. I do not have a goal that encourages me to carry on." Do you ever feel like that? Like you don't have a goal that gives you the drive to keep on going? I was telling the Lord this morning that I feel like that. I feel like my drive is drying up, and only a puddle of it is left over. So I asked Him to multiply my drive into a river. I want it to be mighty and rushing, pushing me forward on swift rapids of inspiration. The problem is, most days when my alarm goes off, I don't have a goal that encourages me to carry on. Nothing drives me. I feel disoriented. Upside down. Lost.

Do you know the feeling I'm talking about? The feeling that you're just taking up space? That you're a pointless human who has no idea why you were put on planet earth to begin with?

Here, at the end of this book, I'm going to share with you the thing I am the most passionate about. I'm going to tell you a secret . . .

I've found the cure to emptiness.

I know that may sound absurdly presumptuous and overconfident. But it's true. I've found the answer to every one of my problems. I have a secret compass that gives me direction whenever I'm wandering through life entirely lost.

I remember when I was eighteen years old, I was the most lost I'd ever been. Not emotionally, but literally. I was moving from San Diego to Medford, Oregon, so I stuffed all my belongings into my Jeep and headed north. Instead of taking the 5 freeway, though, I decided to take the 101, because the 101 would lead me through the Redwoods. Ever since I was in about 5th grade, I had wanted to take a trip back to that beautiful forest. Besides, they filmed *Return of the Jedi* there, so I just couldn't pass up this opportunity!

When I finally reached the Avenue of the Giants, the road that goes through sky-scraping trees, I pulled over because I spotted a nice hiking trail. I got out, locked my car (or more literally, my moving house) and headed deep into the forest.

It was awesome. I was having a blast hanging out, just me, Jesus, and the redwood trees. But all of a sudden, in the middle of my hike, I came to a fork in the road. I went right because that was the trail that led further into the woods. So I continued on my journey, enjoying every minute of my beautiful hike. But before long the sun began to set, it was getting cold, and I was starting to get a little freaked out. Right about then I decided to head back to my Jeep.

But as I was heading back, I came to that same fork in the road. This is where things started getting bad. I couldn't remember for the life of me which way I was supposed to go. I should've been like Hansel and Gretel and left a trail of crumbs or something (only that didn't work out too well for them either) because I had no clue where I was. But I had to make up my mind and try *something*, so I tried a left. The only problem with the left was it led me in one giant circle back to the fork. Then I took a right, but right only led me further into the forest. I started to panic. Neither direction was taking me back to my car. It was getting late and I had no idea what wild beasts might be roaming around at this hour. So I decided to take matters into my own hands. I forsook the path entirely and figured I could blaze my own trail. Who needs trails anyways?

So there I was, in the middle of the forest, completely disoriented, trying to find my way without a path. After a while I realized this wasn't working. So what do I do? I stop for a moment and pause to think, and then I just start booking it. I start sprinting through the woods. If someone saw me they'd think I was crazy, but I was desperate. Of course, sprinting wildly through the forest only got me more and more lost. But suddenly I remembered something. I had my cell phone in my pocket! At that time those Verizon commercials were on TV where the guy walked around and asked "Can you hear me now?" I had Verizon, and I was *really* hoping someone would be able to hear me now more than ever.

I busted out my cell phone, and for the first time in my life, I dialed 911. You wouldn't think there'd be service in the middle of the woods, but somehow, praise the Lord, there was. A lady answered the phone and said, "This is 911, what's your emergency?" I said, "My name's Ben. I'm in the forest somewhere in California. I don't know where I am. How do I get back to my car?" The lady then connected me to the local park rangers. Nicole the Park Ranger came on the line and said, "Hi, you're lost in the forest somewhere in California. Can you tell me specifically where you're at?" I look around and observe for a moment, then answer, "I'm next to a bunch of trees!" I don't think that helped very much, but somehow she and Allen (her fellow park ranger) were able to drive around and find my Jeep.

Allen got out of his car and began searching for me. He started hooping and hollering, maybe making a bird sound here and there, and I hoop and holler back. Sure enough, after a while of making noises at each other, he was able to find me.

Then the most amazing thing happened. Allen, *without a compass, navigational system, or even a trail,* led me straight back to my car from the middle of the forest! It was crazy. I couldn't figure out how he did it. He was even making friendly conversation with me as he effortlessly took me back to my car from the middle of nowhere. It blew my mind.

Jesus is just like Allen the Park Ranger in the story. When we have no idea where we're going in life, it's okay, because all we have to do is follow Him around. *He* knows where He's going, so as long as we stay close to Him, we'll just happen to end up at our destination! He will lead us to where we want to go, no problem! Yet so often we try to find our own way through different paths and formulas, or we try to blaze our own trails, but we always end up lost. Shia LaBeouf tried acting, Chris Martin tried music, and Tom Brady tried football, but they've found that all these paths in and of themselves lead nowhere. That's why Jesus claimed He *is* the trail (John 14:6), and until we realize that He is the way to our destiny, we'll just get more and more lost and confused.

I love how in Jeremiah 33:3, God promised that if we call on Him He will answer. When I dialed 911, I knew they'd answer and come to my rescue. So too, when we call the Lord, we can know for a fact He will answer and rescue us every time. We never get His voicemail.

My friend Nick Griffin knows this well. When you call him and he doesn't pick up, his voice comes on and says, "Hi you've reached Nicholas Griffin. You called upon me, and I did not answer. If you call upon Jesus the Risen Christ, He will always answer. God bless your day. I love you." Isn't that awesome? Even though millions of people are calling Jesus right now, He always picks up. And He miraculously can give each of us His undivided attention. So let's grab our spiritual cell phones and pray for crying out loud, and we'll be rescued at last!

Did you know that in 1 Thessalonians 5:17 we are literally told to *pray without ceasing?* The question is, how in the world do we pray without stopping? My brother Peter-John answered this question beautifully in a teaching he gave several years back. You know when you really like a girl, and you're talking on the phone with her late into the night? Eventually you realize it's time to go, so you say goodbye. But you don't hang up the phone. And she doesn't either. She says she won't go until you hang up, but then you say, "No, you hang up first!" And for an hour you debate about who should hang up first and you never really get off the phone. Sometimes you even fall asleep with the phone to your ear. That's how it should be with Jesus. We talk to Him so much that we never really hang up the phone. We're just in an on-going, non-stop conversation with Him throughout the day.

It's no wonder Jesus said to His disciples, "I no longer call you servants . . . instead I call you friends." *He wants to talk with us the same way best friends talk.* That's why my favorite thing to do is to go on walks with Jesus. I love to walk through the city at night and just talk to Him. I may look like a crazy person to cars driving by, but who cares? It's just too good to pass up. The funny thing is that I don't pray noble things or deeply spiritual prayers. I just tell Him what's on my heart. What I'm inspired by. What I'm struggling with. What I'm confused about. I'll ask Him questions. And He *always* answers my calls. I leave my home in despair, and when I get back from my walk I'm ridiculously happy. Ask Necia. It's crazy. And not only that, but after my prayer walks He will change my circumstances around to line up with the requests I just prayed!

But the problem is a lot of times I fall into the trap of "I spent five minutes with Jesus today so I'm good to go" mentality. Maybe you do that too. We check off our relationship with Jesus from the spiritual To-Do list. But we have to remember that the Bible not only teaches we are His friend, but also His *bride.*

Could you imagine if I came home today and said to Necia, "Neesh, I just had a breakthrough! I read this sweet book about marriage and discovered that if I spend five minutes with you every day, we'll have a great relationship!" So let's say we spent five minutes together, then I said, "seeya later love!" She probably wouldn't be too happy about that. In order to have a strong relationship, we should be hanging out whenever we get a chance. And it's no different in our marriage relationship with Christ.

I guarantee you, if every day you have a non-stop, ongoing friendship with Jesus, you will end up being the happiest person on the planet. Psalm 144:15 says, "Happy indeed are those people whose God is the LORD." That's a promise. He doesn't give a superficial happiness that goes away once life starts getting hard. No. He fulfills our deepest longings and will blow our mind with true pleasure when we finally do what we were created for . . . when we bond with our Maker.

"So Ben," you ask, "what is this cure to emptiness you say you've found?"

It's Jesus Christ.

I've found the cure! I know a billion other people have found this cure too, but it's so real to me that I feel as though I'm the only one who knows about it. I feel like I have the cure to cancer, and I just want to tell the world about it. Not because I read it in a book somewhere, but because I've seen it in my life firsthand. I can't explain how He does it, but I come to Jesus a broken mess, and He fixes me. Every time. He fixes me.

He is the answer to every problem I've ever had in life. Period. I don't have five steps that will lead you to a happier life. I don't have a secret formula that will make you a better Christian. I don't have any of those things because those things don't work for me. But Jesus does. Every time. *He's like a flawless calculator that solves every one of my problems and never messes up.* And too often I try to solve life's problems on my own, but the human predicament is like calculus. I can't solve it on my own. When I try to do it all in my head I'm just going to get a headache. But Jesus, well, there's no problem that He can't solve.

He's the way when we're lost in the woods. He's the truth when we have no clue what to believe. He's the life when we're scared to death of dying. And He's the missing puzzle piece in our lives when we're puzzled about what life's all about.

He's the Park Ranger who is my compass when I'm lost. The 911 receptionist who answers my calls and comes to the rescue. *He's* the cure to the emptiness Shia LaBeouf, Tom Brady, Chris Martin, and me and you feel, and the Best Friend who will talk to us on the phone for hours on end without ever getting tired of us!

He's the air hole when we finally admit we don't have disinhyperated lungs, and the Mama Giraffe who kicks us so that we learn to stand and continues to do so even when we're angry at Him for it. He's the First Hand Dreamer who breathes "secondhand dreams" into our hearts, and the delicious Candy Tyme snack that delights our hungry soul. He's the Superhero we've been searching for ever since we were kids, and the happy ending to this journey we've taken together . . .

Throughout the roller coaster of hopes and challenges that have twisted and turned through the pages of this book, we've finally come to the end of the ride. And Jesus is right here waiting for us as we fix our wind-blown hair, unbuckle our seatbelts, and step onto the pavement.

Now it's time to take Jesus off the pages of this book, and live for Him with all the vigor we can muster from our young hearts. This is our chance to go big for His kingdom and set the world on fire.

In the movie *Amazing Grace,* when William Pitt the Younger told his friend William Wilberforce that he was going to run for Prime Minister, Wilberforce said, "Billy, no one of our age has ever taken power." Pitt responded, "Which is why we're too young to realize that certain things are impossible, so we will do them anyway." And he did. Pitt became the youngest Prime Minister in British history . . . at the age of twenty-four.

You have dreams. Go and live them for Jesus. If not now, when? I know you may feel too young. I know you don't feel ready. But as Pablo Picasso said, "I am always doing that which I cannot do, in order that I may learn how to do it."

Is there anything in all the world you can't do if Jesus is by your side? When you're old and lying on your deathbed, will you regret your youth because you held back, or will you look back and see your fondest memories because you attempted great things for God? The choice is yours.

I say we rise up to meet our destiny. I say we embrace our fate as a chosen generation, as His own special people. Destined to defeat the darkness. Summoned to His army of light. And the Captain of our Salvation is recruiting those whose commitment is not in lip service only, but in heart, to wage war against the wisdom of the world.

The battle cry sounds. The swords are drawn. The regiments stand still as stone. There's no middle ground. There's no turning back. Now we charge the front lines, marching to the beat of Jesus' heart.

The principalities and powers of evil are about to meet their doom.